How
to
Study

Other books in this Kogan Page series:
Getting Organised
Improve Your Memory
Improve Your Reading
Improve Your Writing
Last Minute Study Tips

Forthcoming
Manage Your Time
Pass Any Test
Take Notes
Use Your Computer

How
to
Study

Ron Fry

**KOGAN
PAGE**

First published in 1996 in the USA by The Career Press,
3 Tice Road, PO Box 687, Franklin Lakes, NJ 07417
This European edition published 1997 by Kogan Page Ltd

Kogan Page Limited
120 Pentonville Road
London N1 9JN

British Library Cataloguing in Publication Data

A CIP record for this book is available from the British Library.

ISBN 0 7494 2351 X

Typeset by Jo Brereton, Primary Focus, Haslington, Cheshire
Printed and bound in Great Britain by Clays Ltd St Ives plc

Contents

INTRODUCTION:
How to use this book

*'What one knows is, in youth, of little moment;
they know enough who know how to learn.'*

HENRY ADAMS

Learning how to study is learning how to learn. And that is, to me, the greatest gift you can ever give yourself.

Having stated that so boldly, I suspect I still have to convince some readers that spending any time trying to master this stuff – studying, reading, note-taking, writing, whatever you call it – is worth your while.

Believe it or not, there are some very good reasons why you *should* learn how to study, why you *must* learn how to study. But before I start convincing you that developing proper study skills really is important, and why, let us work out exactly what we mean by 'study skills' so we are all on the same wavelength.

How to Study includes hints, advice and techniques for taking notes in class, while you are reading your textbooks, in the library or even online, how to prepare for tests and how to organise your study schedule to get the best results in the shortest space of time. But that is the second half of the book. There are essential skills you may think do not even have anything to do with studying, and important steps you need to take right from the start.

Here's where you start

*'Learn as though you would never be able to master it;
hold it as if you would be in fear of losing it.'*
CONFUCIUS

Developing good study habits is like a race between you and your friends around a track. Before you can declare a winner, you have to agree where the finish line is. In other words, how do you measure your ability to use skills? What's good? What's poor?

But you cannot even start the race until you know where the starting line is – especially if it is drawn at a different spot for each of you.

Chapter 1 starts by explaining the study skills and clarifying how each can and should function in your life. Then you have the chance to find your own starting line.

In Chapter 2, you will learn the importance of where, how and when you study and start building the study environment that is perfect for you. Why is this important? If you have spent three hours reading *Ulysses* with Take That shaking the walls, it is not surprising you are still on page three. Reading about and understanding Bloom's day might have little to do with increasing reading comprehension, rescheduling your time or changing books… and a lot more to do with just turning down the volume.

There is no magic elixir in the study habit regime. If maths and science are not your strong points, memorising *How to Study* will not transform you into a Nobel Prize-winning physicist. Nobody is good at everything, but everybody is good at something. So you will also get a chance to rate the subjects you like and dislike, plus those classes you do best and worst in.

Chapter 2 also introduces some of the 'intangibles' in the study equation: your home environment, attitude, motivation, etc. If you are dedicated to studying and motivated to achieve certain goals, all the other factors that affect your study habits will fall more naturally into place. A belief in the study ethic is one of the keys to success.

Finally, some generalities about the study process – learning to understand teachers, developing mentors, dealing with perfectionism, the importance of flexibility – will help you get off to the right start.

Reading and comprehension

Chapter 3 introduces the skills basic to any study process: reading and comprehension. No matter how well you learn to take notes, how familiar you become with your library, how doggedly you study for tests, if you are reading poorly (or not enough) and not understanding what you read, life will be difficult.

Becoming a good reader is a skill, one usually acquired early in life. If it is a skill you have not acquired yet, now is the time. Chapter 3 also points out how your ability to recall ideas, facts and figures can be significantly increased (quantitatively and qualitatively) with the right practice.

Making up for lost time

To see a significant change in your life, many of you will not need to study harder, just more intelligently. This means making better use of your study time – spending the same two, three or four hours, but accomplishing two, three or four times what you do now. Chapter 4 introduces the simplest and easiest-to-use organisational and time management tools – powerful ways to make sure you are always on track, including guidelines to develop both short-term and long-term calendars.

Go to the top of the class

Chapter 5 looks at the one experience we all have in common, no matter how old we are – the classroom. I will help you to take better notes, encourage your active participation in lesson or seminar discussions – including pointers on how to overcome the tendency to hide behind the plant at the back of the room – and get a lot more out of lectures.

Learning about your library

Chapter 6 introduces you to the single most important resource in your study career – your library. You will learn about the books, periodicals, newspapers, magazines, computer software, video and audio tapes and other reference materials available to you, with suggestions for how to find and use them, including an explanation of the Dewey Decimal Classification System.

Surfing now, surfing now...

You may already be computer literate, perhaps even a frequent Net surfer. If you do not know a bit from a byte, you will learn in Chapter 7 how vital it is to master the computer, plus how to buy yours, how to find the Net and what to do when you get there.

So you are not the next Dickens

I'm convinced that too many people place the emphasis in 'writing essays' on the word 'writing'. Chapter 8 introduces you to a remarkably easy way to gather research, take notes and organise your information. By breaking down any written assignment, no matter how complex, into easy-to-follow steps, I think you will find you create essays infinitely better than before – even if you are still no threat to Dickens (or anybody else) when it comes to writing.

How to 'sail through' any test

Chapter 9 covers the dos and don'ts of exam preparation (including the differences between studying for weekly tests, mid-term and final examinations), why last-minute cramming does not work (but how to do it if you have no other choice), studying for and taking different types of tests (multiple-choice, essays, open book, etc), how to increase your guessing scores, even which questions to answer first and which to leave until last.

How well do you study?

How to Study is a comprehensive study guide – a fundamental step-by-step approach that you can follow to develop and sharpen your study skills.

If you are struggling through school, college or university, here's your lifeline.

If you are a secondary school student planning to go on to further education, now is your chance to hone your study skills.

If you are heading for an apprenticeship, planning to dance, write, paint, etc, not considering further education, even if you are ready to leave school at the earliest possible opportunity, you need *How to Study*.

If you are an adult returning to the classroom after a lengthy absence, there is no substitute for the tips and techniques you will learn in this helpful collection.

So what if you are a really poor student? How clever you are is not the point. What counts is how well you study.

With the possible exception of the two per cent of you who qualify as 'gifted', the effective study habits this book teaches will help students of any age.

If your marks are average to good, you will see a definite improvement. If you are on the borderline of the pass/fail range, you will benefit considerably. If good study habits are in place but rusty as a result of years away from the classroom, *How to Study* will be the perfect refresher for you.

And if you *are* one of those gifted two per cent, I still think you will find many helpful techniques in these pages.

Who is the book really for?

While I originally wrote *How to Study* for secondary school students, I have discovered over the years that these students make up only a small proportion of people who actually bought the book. The surprise was that so many of the people buying (and writing many letters to me along the way) were adults. A number of them were returning to further education and saw *How to Study* as a great refresher. Some had left school years ago but had worked out that if they could learn now the study skills their teachers never taught them, they would do better in their careers.

All too many were parents who had the same lament: 'How do I get John/Jane to read (study, do better in tests, remember more, get better marks, etc)?'

So I want to briefly take the time to address each one of the audiences for this book and discuss some of the factors particular to each of you.

If you are a secondary school student

You should be particularly comfortable with the format of the book – its relatively short sentences and paragraphs, occasionally humorous (hopefully) headings and subheadings and the language used. I wrote it with you in mind.

But you should also be uncomfortable with the fact that you are already in the middle of your school years – the period that will drastically affect, one way or the other, all the rest of your education – and you still do not know how to study! Don't lose another minute. Make learning how to study and mastering all of the study skills in this book your absolute priority.

If you are a 'traditional' college or university student

(By 'traditional' I mean somewhere in the 18 to 25 age range), I hope you are tackling one or two of the study skills you failed to master at school. Otherwise, I cannot see how you are ever going to succeed in college. If you are starting from scratch, my advice is the same as to the secondary school students reading this book: drop everything and make it your number one priority.

If you are the parent of a student of any age

Your child's school, college or university is probably doing little if anything to teach him or her how to study, which means he or she is not learning how to learn. And that means he or she is not learning how to succeed.

What can parents do? There are probably even more dedicated parents out there than dedicated students. Here are the rules for parents of students of any age.

1 Set up a homework area. Free of distraction, well lit, all necessary supplies handy.

2 Set up a homework routine. When and where it gets done. Same start time every day.

3 Set homework priorities. Make the point that homework is the priority – before TV, going out with friends or to play, whatever.

4 Make reading a habit – for them, certainly, but also for yourselves, if it is not already. Children will inevitably do what you do, not what you say.

5 Turn off the TV. Or, at the very least, severely limit the amount of TV-watching you do.

6 Talk to the teachers. Find out what your children are supposed to be learning.

7 Encourage and motivate, but do not nag them to do their homework. That does not work.

8 Supervise their work, but do not fall into the trap of doing their homework for them.

9 Praise them to succeed, but do not overpraise them for mediocre work.

10 Convince older students of reality. Learning and believing that the real world does not care about their marks, but measures them solely by what they know and what they can do is a lesson that will save many tears, including yours.

11 If you can afford it, get your children a computer and all the software they can handle. Your children, whatever their age, must master computer technology in order to survive, let alone succeed, in and after school.

The importance of your involvement

Do not for a minute underestimate the importance of your commitment to your child's success: your involvement in your child's education is absolutely essential to his or her eventual success.

So please, take the time to read this book. Learn what your children should be learning. You can help tremendously, even if you were not a brilliant student yourself, even if you never learned good study skills. You can learn now with your child – not only will it help him or her at school, it will also help you in your job, whatever your field.

If you are a non-traditional student

If you are going back to further education at the age of 25, 45, 65 or 85 – you probably need the help in *How to Study* more than anyone. Why? Because the longer you have been out of education, the more likely it is that you do not remember what you have forgotten – and you have forgotten what you are supposed to remember. As much as I emphasise that it is rarely too early to learn good study habits, I must also emphasise that it is never too late.

What you won't find in this book

I have seen so-called study books spend chapters on proper nutrition, how to dress, how to exercise and a number of other topics that are not covered at all in *How to Study*, except for this briefest of all acknowledgements: it is inevitable that diet, sleep, exercise, use of drugs (including nicotine and caffeine) and alcohol all affect studying, perhaps significantly.

Having said that, I see little reason to waste your time detailing what should be obvious. Anything – including studying – is more difficult if you are hungry, unhealthy, hungover, etc. So please use common sense. Ensure your eating is as healthy as it can be, get whatever sleep your body requires, stay reasonably fit and avoid alcohol and drugs. If your lack of success is in any way due to one of these other factors and you are unable to deal with it alone, find a good book or a professional to help you.

1 *Starting off on the right foot*

> *'It is not enough to understand what we ought to be, unless we understand what we are; and we do not understand what we are, unless we know what we ought to be.'*
>
> T S ELIOT

Taking a good, honest look at yourself is not the easiest thing in the world. In the next two chapters, I am going to help you evaluate the current level of all your study skills, a necessary step to identify the areas in which you need to concentrate your efforts; identify the study environment and learning style that suit you; and categorise all of your school subjects according to how much you enjoy them and how well you do in them.

How to keep score

In the next few pages, I will explain the 11 primary study skills covered in this book: reading and comprehension, memory development (retention), time management, library skills, computer skills, textbook note-taking, classroom note-taking, library note-taking, classroom participation, writing essays and test preparation. Then I will ask you to rate yourself on your current level of achievement and understanding of these skills: A for mastery or near mastery of a particular skill; B for some mastery; C for little or none.

Remember: There are no right or wrong answers in this assessment. It is only a place to start, a jumping-off point from which you can measure your progress and rate those areas in which your skills need improvement.

To simplify the process, I have listed the primary study skills on page 10. Take a separate piece of paper and rate yourself on each of the 11 skills (from reading to test preparation) before you read the rest of this chapter. After you have rated yourself in each area, give yourself two points for every A, one point for every B, no points for every C. If your overall rating is 18 or more, excellent (give yourself an A); 13 to 17, good (give yourself a B); and if 12 or less, fair (give yourself a C). Mark this rating under Initial Study Skills Evaluation.

Now, let us review each of these areas, giving you insight as to what 'fair', 'good' and 'excellent' really mean. As you read each section, fill in your rating on the Your Starting Point chart – and be honest with yourself. This evaluation will give you a benchmark from which to measure your improvement after you have completed the book. File it away and make the comparison when you have finished reading.

Your Starting Point

Initial Study Skills Evaluation	A [ ]	B [ ]	C [ ]
Reading	A [ ]	B [ ]	C [ ]
Memory development	A [ ]	B [ ]	C [ ]
Time management	A [ ]	B [ ]	C [ ]
Basic library skills	A [ ]	B [ ]	C [ ]
Computer skills	A [ ]	B [ ]	C [ ]
Textbook note-taking	A [ ]	B [ ]	C [ ]
Classroom note-taking	A [ ]	B [ ]	C [ ]
Library note-taking	A [ ]	B [ ]	C [ ]
Classroom participation	A [ ]	B [ ]	C [ ]
Writing essays	A [ ]	B [ ]	C [ ]
Test preparation	A [ ]	B [ ]	C [ ]
Overall Study Skills Level	A [ ]	B [ ]	C [ ]

Reading

Speed, comprehension and recall are the three important components of reading. Comprehension and recall are especially interrelated – better to sacrifice some speed to increase these two factors. To test your reading and comprehension skills, read the passage below, close the book and jot down what you think were the key points. Then review the text and compare your notes with the passage. You will get a good idea of how well you understood what you read and just how good your top-of-the-mind recall is.

Five major scandals tainted the administration of President Ulysses S Grant. Although the hero of Vicksburg was the first president to encounter charges of substantial wrongdoing during his administration, it was never proved that he was directly involved in any criminal acts nor that he profited from any of the acts of others.

The first incident occurred in 1869, the first year of his presidency. Known as Black Friday, it involved speculators James Fisk and Jay Gould and their attempt to corner the gold market. President Grant was not directly involved in Fisk's and Gould's machinations, but he gave the appearance of complicity, allowing himself to be entertained lavishly and publicly on Fisk's yacht.

The second major scandal involved the embezzlement of massive amounts of money by the Credit Mobilier holding company, which was involved with the construction of the Union Pacific railway. To avoid being discovered, the conspirators heavily bribed Congressmen and officials of the Republican Party, of which Grant was the nominal head.

Two other scandals involved taxes and officials appointed to collect them. One tax collector, John Sanborn, managed to keep nearly half of the delinquent taxes he collected, a total exceeding $200,000. That paled in comparison to the fraud discovered by Treasury Secretary Benjamin H Bristow among liquor distillers and the officials charged with collecting taxes from them. Although Grant called for swift action against the conspirators, his fervour flagged when his trusted personal secretary, Orville Babcock, was implicated in the scheme. Grant then slowed the investigation, but 110 conspirators were eventually found guilty.

In the final year of Grant's second term, evidence mounted that Secretary of War W W Belknap had been taking bribes from white traders at Indian trading posts. Faced with certain impeachment, Belknap resigned.

Score: If you can read the material straight through and accurately summarise what you have read, all in less than two minutes, give yourself an A. If you have some problems reading and understanding the text but are able to complete the assignment in less than four minutes, give yourself a B. If you are unable to complete the assignment in that time, remember what you read or produce accurate notes at all, give yourself a C.

Retention

There are various methods to help you recall when you must remember a lot of specific facts. One of these is memorising – committing information to word-for-word recall. Memorise only when you are required to remember something for a relatively short time.

Test No. 1: Look at the number following this paragraph for 10 seconds. Then cover the page and write down as much of it as you can remember.

762049582049736

Test No. 2: At the top of the next page are 12 nonsense words from a language I made up and their 'definitions'. Study the list for 60 seconds in an attempt to remember each word, how it is spelled and its definition.

Bruhe	Arm	**Trouch**	Vomit
Imbor	Worry	**Laved**	Woman
Timp	Brother	**Yout**	Toe
Batoe	Walker	**Frewie**	Cupboard
Plitter	Chin	**Slecum**	Trousers
Kruk	Bathroom	**Preb**	Shout

Close the book and write down each of the 12 words and its definition. They do not need to be in the order in which they were listed.

Score:
Test No. 1: If you remembered 12 or more digits in the correct order, give yourself an A, 8–12, a B; seven or less, a C.

Test No. 2: If you accurately listed eight or more words and definitions (and that includes spelling my new words correctly) – A. If you listed from five to seven words and their definitions, or correctly listed and spelled more than eight words but mixed up their definitions – B. If you were unable to remember at least four words and their definitions – C.

Time management

Your effective use of available study time can be measured by two yardsticks:

1 your ability to break down assignments into component parts (eg, reading, note-taking, outlining, writing); and

2 your ability to complete each task in an efficient manner.

Score: If you feel you use your time wisely and efficiently – A. If you know there are times when you simply run out of time – B. If you cannot tell the time – C.

Library skills

Making the most of the library is a function of understanding its organisation – and using it. The more time you spend there – studying, reading, researching – the more productive you will be. You will become adept at tracking down reference materials and finding the information you need quickly.

Virtually all libraries follow the same organisation – once you understand it you will be 'library literate', no matter which library you use. In this book, you will discover what kinds of resources are available (books, periodicals, directories, encyclopaedias, dictionaries, magazines, newspapers, documents, microfilm files), you will learn how to select and find books (learning the Dewey Decimal System) and you will find out about the functions of the library staff.

To evaluate your library skills, answer the following questions.

1 What collections are restricted in your library?

2 Where would you find a biography of Winston Churchill in your local library?

3 Where is the reference section in your local library?

4 Given the Dewey number for a book, could you find it in less than five minutes?

5 How often have you been to the library in the past six months? The past month?

Score: If the answers to these questions are all obvious to you, indicating a steady pattern of library use, then you can claim to have the library habit – A. If you cannot answer one or more of the questions or freely own up to a casual record of library use – B. If you do not have the faintest idea of where the closest library is, give yourself a C.

Computer skills

It is virtually impossible now to succeed at almost any level of education without complete mastery of the computer. But knowing how to use a computer, modem and scanner is just the beginning. You have to know how to use them to study both more efficiently and effectively. That includes learning how to write better essays and keep to your schedules, and taking advantage of the almost limitless research possibilities available online.

Score: If you are capable of doing just about anything online short of hacking into the Ministry of Defence and have made computer equipment a key tool in your quest for more efficient studying and better marks, score an A. If you are adept at word processing and playing games and at least can get online, but have never used 75 per cent of the other tools on your computer and 'wipe out' more often than surf – B. If you do not even know what 'being online' means and need four minutes to work out how to turn the computer on – C.

Note-taking

Three different arenas – at home with textbooks, in the classroom, at the library – require different methods of note-taking.

From textbooks. Working from your books at home, you should identify the main ideas, rephrasing information in your own words, as well as capturing the details with which you were unfamiliar. Take brief, concise notes in a separate notebook as you read. Write down questions and answers to ensure your mastery of the material, highlighting those questions to which you do not have answers so you can ask them in class.

In the classroom. Class preparation is the key to class participation. By reading material to be covered before you come to the classroom, you will be able to concentrate and absorb the teacher's interpretations and points. Using a topical, short sentence approach or your own shorthand or symbols, take notes on those items that will trigger thematic comprehension of the subject matter. These notes should be sequential, following the teacher's lecture pattern. After the lesson, review your notes at the first opportunity and fill in any blanks and your own thoughts.

In the library. What is the difference between taking notes at the library or working at home with library books versus your own textbooks? Sooner or later you will have to return library books (if you are allowed to take them out at all), and librarians discourage highlighting them, so you need an effective system for library note-taking, see Chapter 6.

Score: If you feel that your note-taking skills are sufficient to summarise the necessary data from your textbooks and capture the key points from classroom, lectures and discussions, and they allow you to prepare detailed outlines and write good essays, score an A. If you feel any one of these three areas is deficient – B. If notes are what you pass to your friends in class – C.

Participating in the classroom

I do not know that many teachers who do not take each student's classroom or seminar participation into account when giving marks, no matter how many spot tests they put on or how many essays they assign. Also, you may have discovered, there are teachers out there who will mark down students who do well in every essay and test if they seem to disappear in the classroom.

Score: If you are always prepared for lessons (which means, at the very least, reading all assigned material, preparing assigned homework and projects and handing them in on time), actively participate in discussions and ask frequent and pertinent questions as a way of both showing what you already know and filling in the gaps in that knowledge, give yourself an A. If you fail in any of these criteria – B. If you are not sure where the classroom is, score C.

Writing essays

Preparing any sort of report, written or oral, is 90 per cent perspiration (research) and 10 per cent inspiration (writing). In other words, the ability to write a good essay is more dependent on your mastery of the other skills we have already discussed than your mastery of writing. If you are an avid reader, familiar with your local library, a good note-taker and capable of breaking down the most complex topic into the manageable steps necessary to write an essay, you probably turn in superior essays.

Score: If you have already given yourself an A in library skills, library note-taking, time management and reading, score A. If you feel you turn in relatively good papers but are lacking in any of these areas – B. If your idea of writing a paper is photocopying the pertinent 'Letts Notes' and recopying the summary in your own handwriting – C.

Exam and test preparation

The key to proper exam and test preparation is an accurate assessment of what material will be covered and what form the exam will take. Weekly class tests usually cover the most recent material. Mid-term and final examinations cover a much broader area – usually all the subject matter to date. Multiple-choice tests, essays, lists of maths problems, science lab tests all require different preparation and the application of different test-taking skills. Knowing the kind of test you are facing will make your preparation much easier.

So will creating your own list of questions you think your teacher will most likely ask. Through periodic review of your text and lesson notes, the areas in which your teacher appears most interested – and on which he or she is most likely to test you – should begin to stand out. As a final trick, prepare a list of 10 or more questions you would ask if the roles were reversed and you were the teacher.

Score: If you are able to construct tests that are harder than the ones your teacher gives you – and you perform well on those, score A. If you feel you know the material, but somehow do not perform as well as you think you should at test time – B. If you forget you are having a test, give yourself a C.

Your overall score

Once again, after you have rated yourself in each area, give yourself two points for every A, one point for every B, no points for every C. If your overall rating is 18 or more, excellent (give yourself an A); 13–17, good (give yourself a B); and if 12 or less, fair (give yourself a C). Put your new score in the section Overall Study Skills Level in the chart on page10.

Now what?

The fact that you have been honest with yourself in evaluating those talents you bring into the study game is a big plus in your favour. Knowing where you are strong and where you need to improve makes everything else a good deal easier. Now, based on your test results, draw up a list of your assets and liabilities – your areas of strength and weakness. This will focus your attention on those areas that will require the most work for improvement.

While I would strongly recommend you read the entire book, this simple test has enabled you to identify the chapters you really need to work on and the specific skills that may require work long after you finish reading this book.

2 How to organise your studying

What effect can good study habits have? Certainly natural talents and skills – the basic abilities you were born with – have the most to do with success in school, 50 per cent, maybe 60. The environment in which you are trying to learn, your health and other such factors may be another 10 per cent, maybe 15. That leaves 25–40 per cent for study skills.

You do not believe that learning how to study can have such a huge effect? Two comments: first, read this book, practise the skills, watch the results. I think you will discover I am right. Second, if you do not believe study skills are so important, you must be giving more weight to ability, kind of a 'bright people do well because they are bright' approach. Well, a lot of bright people do not do well. Others do well in school but test poorly. Many are good in some subjects and not so good in others. Look at your friends, at others in your school, and I guarantee you will prove it to yourself.

What kind of effort are we talking about here? Another hour a night? Two hours a night? More? 'If I'm studying longer', you might reasonably contend, 'I am surely studying harder, at least by my definition'.

Take the latter point first. You can study more effectively. You can put in less time and get better results. But learning how to do so is hard, because learning of any kind takes discipline and learning self-discipline is, to many of us, the most difficult task of all. So do not fool yourself. You are not going to sit down, read *How to Study*, and suddenly transform yourself from a C student to an A student. But you can make the transformation if you put in the time to learn the lessons this book contains and, more importantly, practise and use them every day.

If you are currently doing little or no work towards your education, then you are going to have to put in more time and effort. How much more? Or even more generally, how long should you study? Until you get the results you want to achieve. The smarter you are and the more easily you learn and adapt the techniques in this book, the more likely you will be spending less time on your assignments than before. But the further you need to go – from Ds to As rather than Bs to As – the more you need to learn and the longer you need to give yourself to learn it.

Do not get discouraged. You will see results surprisingly quickly.

Make study habit-forming

If you are doing poorly at school and you are actually putting in a reasonable amount of study time, you have got poor study habits and failure has, to some extent, become a habit.

This is good news, as not only can bad habits be broken, but they can be replaced by good habits relatively easily. Here is your plan.

▮ It is much easier to replace one of your habits than to break it entirely. So do not attempt to stop poor study habits, just learn the good ones that substitute for them.

▮ Practise, practise, practise. There is no way around it, practice is the motor oil that lubricates any habit's engine. The more you do something, the more ingrained it becomes. Just ask any smoker how many times he lit a cigarette today without even noticing that he had done so.

▮ Tell your friends and family of your decision to do better at school by honing your study skills. This works for some people, who find that the added pressure is a good motivator. For some of you, however, such a strategy simply adds too much pressure and is more likely to backfire instead, encouraging failure. My advice would be to use such a strategy if you know it will help you personally, avoid it if you know it will actually hurt.

▌ You do not have to struggle from Ds to As with no feed-back. Obviously, there is a lot of distance for you to travel and you will be seeing the effects of better study habits all along the way. Each effect you see just strengthens your re-solve and makes it even easier to keep on going. To make sure you get a 'motivational jolt' from every accomplish-ment, resolve to chart every inch of your progress. You may want to set up a chart on your wall on which you list 'To-day's Successes' every day. Remember the small steps you are taking – saving five minutes on a reading assignment, finding the books you need at the library more quickly, feel-ing that you took good notes in a lecture, raising your hand to actually answer a teacher's question in a classroom dis-cussion, etc.

Starting with the next chapter, everything in this book will concentrate on specific strategies useful for specific tasks – writing papers, note-taking, test-taking, reading, etc. So this is probably the best place to discuss some overall study strate-gies that have little to do with any particular task and everything to do with achieving overall study success.

Get ready to become a 'lifer'

Learning how to study is really a long-term process. Once you undertake the journey, you will be surprised at the number of landmarks, pathways, side streets and road signs you will find. Even after you have transformed yourself into a better student than you had ever hoped to be, you will inevitably find one more signpost that offers new information, one more pathway that leads you in an interesting new direction. Consider learn-ing how to study as a lifelong process and be ready to modify anything you are doing as you learn another method.

This is especially important right from the start when you consider your overall study strategies. How long you study each night, how long you work on a particular subject and how often you schedule breaks are going to vary considerably, depending on how well you were doing before you read this book, how far you have to go, how interested you are in getting there, how involved you are in other activities, the time of day, your general health, etc.

It gets more complicated. What is your study sequence? Hardest assignments first? Easiest? Longest? Shortest? Are you comfortable switching back and forth from one to another or do you need to focus on a single assignment from start to finish?

This gets even more difficult when you consider that the tasks themselves may have a great effect on your schedule. When I sit down to plan out the chapter of a book, for example, I need a relatively long period of uninterrupted time – at least an hour, perhaps three hours – in order to get my notes in the order I want them and to think through the entire chapter, writing transitions in my head, noting problem areas, working out where I need an example or illustration. If I only have half an hour before a meeting or appointment, I would not even attempt to begin such a project, as I would have to start all over again when I had enough time.

You may work in a similar way and, therefore, need to ensure your schedule is flexible enough to adapt to the demands of the specific task. Fifteen-minute study units might work well for you most of the time (though I suspect half an hour is an ideal unit for most of you, an hour only for those of you who can work that long without a break and who have assignments that traditionally take that long to complete).

On the other hand, you may have no problem at all working on a long project in fits and starts, 15 or 20 minutes at a time, without needing to retrace your steps each time you pick it up again.

What is the lesson in all of this? There is no ideal answer, certainly no 'right' answer, to many of the questions I have posed. It is a message you will read in these pages over and over again: find out what works for you and keep on doing it. If it later stops working or does not seem to be working as well, change it.

None of the study techniques discussed in this book is carved in stone. You should feel free to adapt and shape and bend them to your own needs.

Follow the Yellow Brick Road

When I talk about test-taking, one of the key bits of advice is to read the instructions before you start the test. This helps you avoid the poor mark (not to mention the frustration and embarrassment) that results from trying to answer all six essay questions in an hour when you were only supposed to pick three.

Exams are not the only time when 'reading the instructions' is important. Many teachers have their own rules and regulations about handing in homework assignments, preparing essays or projects, reporting lab results, etc. It is just as important to follow these instructions – and just as devastating if you do not.

Be proud of your work... and show it

Do you know any students who make sure they count every word on their 500-word assignment and bring it to a conclusion as fast as they can when they reach that magic number?

How about the student who is convinced his spidery handwriting is perfectly decipherable, even when the teacher has to wade through several deletions on every page and follow arrows from one page to another because the student thought the order should be changed.

Or those who only spell one thing correctly in each essay, or spell a word correctly two or three times and incorrectly four or five others, all on the same page?

Teachers are human. They respond to presentation. While I am not advocating an emphasis on visual impact over content, you should certainly consider that if the substance of two essays or tests or projects is relatively equal, the way in which they are presented may well affect the mark, perhaps significantly.

Besides, there are a lot of teachers who make it a point to give lower grades because of poor grammar, spelling, presentation, etc. And there are others who may subconsciously give higher marks – or give a better mark than the work really warrants – because the presentation was done with care and a sense of pride.

Know your teachers

Teachers are different, too, in their approach to their subjects, their expectations, standards, flexibility, etc. It certainly is worth the effort to compile a 'profile' of each of your teachers. What do each of them want to see in terms of notes, level of participation, essays, projects? What are their individual likes and dislikes? Their methods of grading and testing?

Knowing these various traits can certainly lead you to some adaptation of your approach to each lesson. For example, it is 11pm, you are well past your study prime and you still have reading assignments to complete for English and history tomorrow morning.

The English teacher demands maximum classroom participation and makes it a large part of your final grade – regardless of your test marks. Her hobby seems to be calling on the unprepared, and she has an uncanny and unerring knack for ferreting them out.

The history teacher discourages discussion, preferring to lecture and answer a couple of questions at the end of the lesson. He never asks anyone for anything. Given this situation, and knowing you can stay awake long enough to read only one of the two assignments, which would it be?

Presuming you care at all about your studies and marks, would there ever be a time, barring a simultaneous hurricane, eclipse and bank holiday, that you would go to that English lesson unprepared?

While I will show you in Chapter 4 how to ensure that poor scheduling does not become a habit that leads to such choices, I suspect far too many of you do not take the natural differences among your various teachers into account when planning homework, preparing essays or studying for exams.

Also, I suspect far too few of you try to create a bond with one special teacher – a mentoring relationship – that could well help you avoid some of the bumps and swerves and enable you to reach your goal with far less trouble. Why should you go out of your way to find a mentor? Because you probably need more help – in life, not just in school – than your friends or parents can provide. A mentor can give you that perspective, advice and help.

Intrinsic and extrinsic motivation

Motivators are either intrinsic or extrinsic. What is the difference? You enrol on a voice course. While the hours are certainly necessary to your timetable requirements, you attend the lessons because you love singing – you also have to study biology. You hate the thought of dissecting frogs, and you could not care less whether they have exoskeletons, endoskeletons, hydroskeletons or no skeletons at all, but the course is required.

In the first case, you are motivated by intrinsic factors – you are taking the voice course simply because you truly enjoy it.

The second scenario is an example of extrinsic motivation. While you have no interest in biology, your reward for taking the course is external – you will have completed a science course.

Extrinsic motivation can help you make it through boring or unpleasant tasks that are part of the process of reaching your goals. A vivid image of your final goal can be a powerful motivating force. One student thought about what his job as a computer programmer would be like whenever he needed some help getting through lectures.

Try imagining what a day in your life will be like five or ten years from now. If you have not the faintest idea, no wonder you are having a hard time motivating yourself to work towards that career as a final goal.

The goal pyramid

One way to easily visualise all your goals – and their relation to each other – is to construct a goal pyramid.

1 Centred at the top of a piece of paper, write down what you hope to ultimately gain from your education. This is your long-range goal and the pinnacle of your pyramid. Example: Become a successful advertising copywriter.

2 Below your long-range goal(s), list mid-range milestones or steps that will lead you to your eventual target. For example, if your long-range goal were to become an advertising copywriter, your mid-range goals might include

going to college, getting As for all your writing courses, completing all required courses and getting a summer work placement at a major ad agency.

3 Below the mid-range goals, list as many short-range goals as you can – smaller steps that can be completed in a relatively short period of time. For example, if your long-range goal is to become a travel writer for a widely read magazine, your mid-range goal may be to gain a journalism degree. Short-range goals may include writing a travel article to submit to the school magazine, registering for writing courses or getting an excellent grade in a related class.

Change your goal pyramid as you progress through school. You may eventually decide on a different career. Or your mid-range goals may change as you decide on a different path leading to the long-range goal. The short-range goals will undoubtedly change, even daily.

The process of creating your own goal pyramid allows you to see how all those little daily and weekly steps you take can lead to your mid-range and long-term goals, and will motivate you to work on your daily and weekly tasks with more energy and enthusiasm.

Make goal-setting a part of your life

The development of good study skills is the route to your goals, whatever they are. And no matter how hard you have to work, or how much adversity you have to overcome along the way, the journey will indeed be worth it.

How do you make setting goals a part of your life? Here are some hints that may help.

1 **Be realistic when you set goals.** Do not aim too high or too low and do not be particularly concerned when (not if) you have to make adjustments along the way.

2 **Be realistic about your expectations.** An improved understanding of a subject you have little aptitude for is preferable

to getting hopelessly bogged down if total mastery of the subject is impossible.

3 **Do not give up too easily.** You can be overly realistic – too ready to give up just because something is a trifle harder than you would like. Do not aim too high and feel miserable when you do not come close, or aim too low and never achieve your potential – find the path that is right for you.

4 **Concentrate on areas that offer the best chance for improvement.** Unexpected successes can do wonders for your confidence and might make it possible for you to achieve more than you thought you could even in other areas.

5 **Monitor your achievements and keep resetting your goals.** Daily, weekly, monthly, yearly – ask yourself how you have done and where you would like to go now.

Use rewards as artificial motivators

The way you decide to use a reward system all depends on how much help you need to get motivated to study. As we have observed, tasks that are intrinsically interesting require little outside motivation. However, most work can be spurred along by the promise of small rewards along the way. If the task is especially tedious or difficult, make the rewards more frequent so that motivation does not flag.

As a general rule, the size of the reward should match the difficulty of the task. For an hour of reading, promise yourself a 10-minute walk. For completion of a rough draft for a big assignment, treat yourself to a video.

How perfect are you?

What is a perfectionist and are you one? And if you are, why is it a problem?

Remember the earlier discussion about 'showing you care' and taking the time to 'do things right'? Perfectionists care perhaps too much, finding it impossible to be satisfied with anything less than 'perfect' work (as they define it), presuming for a moment that such an ideal can actually be attained.

It is possible, of course, to score a perfect 100 on a test or to get an A+ on an essay the teacher calls 'perfect' in the margin. But in reality, doing anything perfectly is an impossible task.

What does all this have to do with you? Nothing, unless you find yourself spending two hours polishing an already A+ essay or half an hour searching for that one perfect word or an hour rewriting good notes to make them absolutely perfect. In other words, while striving for perfection may well be a noble characteristic, it can very easily, perhaps inevitably, become a major problem if it becomes an uncontrollable and unstoppable urge that seriously inhibits your enjoyment of your work and your life.

Take it from a perfectionist. It is easy (although still not necessarily good) to be a perfectionist when you are in primary and junior school. But just try to attend lectures and labs (as I did) 38 hours a week, work nearly full time and, of course, do 50+ hours of homework each week, all while wasting days searching for that perfect word. There comes a time – hopefully, for your sake, sooner rather than later – when you must simply conclude that you cannot afford to be a perfectionist. Taking two hours to make an essay perfect when the three word changes you decided upon made no difference to your mark (or the calibre of your work or your understanding of the subject) is a big waste of time.

I am convinced that there are not too many of you out there nodding your head and thinking, 'Oh, yeah, that's me'. But I am equally convinced that those of you to whom this all makes sense are making your lives incredibly tough. If you are a perfectionist – a little or a lot – recognise that characteristic and take the necessary steps to rein it in when you want (or need) to. If you really would prefer spending another couple of hours polishing that A+ paper rather than watching a video, reading a book or getting some other assignment done, be my guest.

Creating your study environment

The time is 9.30pm. Your latest CD is on. Books and notes are strewn across the floor in no particular order. The history test is at 9am tomorrow and you have not looked at the textbook for a week. You have promised your mother you will do the washing up and take the dog for a walk. You were up late watching a favourite TV programme last night and you are still tired.

With all these distractions, the noise level, other commitments and your general tiredness, you are not exactly heading for quality study time. That is the point: within such an environment, time spent will most likely be time wasted. How will you concentrate with loud music? How will you focus on the retention, recognition and recall process when your eyelids are closing? Will you be called away at a critical moment to walk the dog?

Now imagine the following scenario. You have found a quiet corner at a reading table in your local library. You have just finished a lecture and plan to review your history notes while they are still fresh in your mind. You look around you. All heads are down – focusing, concentrating, thinking. This is a study environment – you are not separated from the activities of others, but are a willing participant in a seemingly universal pattern. Now you are ready for quality study time.

In half the time you had planned, you finish your reading, sift the material, make your notes and go home.

This comparison of good and bad study environments is so simple as to be self-evident. Amazingly, the negative situation portrayed is all too often the case. If it is one you are more familiar with, it is time to change. You need the right skills and the right environment if you are to be successful. But the right environment for you is probably the wrong one for someone else. Do you know where, when and how you study best?

In the library? At home? At a friend's? Before dinner? After dinner? When it's quiet? Noisy? With music? With the TV on? Easiest assignments first? Hardest? Reading before writing?

Check it out

On pages 32–3 there is a checklist for you to rate your study environment. It includes not only where you study – at home, in the library, at a friend's – but also when and how you study.

Once you have identified what works for you, avoid those situations in which you know you do not perform best. If you do not know the answer to one or more of the questions, take the time to experiment.

Many of the items on this chart should be understandable by you now. Why you feel the need for a particular environment is not important. Knowing you have a preference is. The following is what you are trying to assess in each item.

1 If you prefer 'listening' to 'seeing', you will have little problem getting the information you need from classroom lectures and discussion. In fact, you will prefer them to studying your textbooks. (You may have to concentrate on your reading skills and spend more time with your textbooks to offset this tendency. Highlighting your texts may help.)

   If you are more of a 'visual' person, you will probably find it easier reading your textbook and may have to work to improve your classroom concentration. Taking excellent lecture notes that you can read later will probably be important for you. You will also want to adapt your note-taking methods to your visual preference – rather than writing notes like everybody else, draw pictures, use charts and learn how to 'map' a lecture. (See Chapters 5 and 8 for a complete discussion of note-taking techniques.)

2 This should tie in with your answer to point 1. The more 'aural' you are, the more you should concentrate on listening. The more 'visual', the better your notes should be for later review.

3 This may make a difference for a number of reasons. You may find it difficult to hear or see from the back of the classroom. You may be shy and want to sit at the front to motivate yourself to participate in discussions. You may find sitting near a window makes you feel a little less claustrophobic; alternatively, you may daydream too much if near a window and should sit as far inside the classroom as possible.

4 Whatever location you find most conducive to study (considering the limitations of your current living situation and schedule) should be where you spend most of your study time.

5 How to organise your time most effectively to cover the material may depend, to a certain extent, on the amount of homework you are burdened with and/or the time of year. You may have one schedule during most of the academic year but have to adapt during exam time, if essays are due, for special projects, etc.

6 To some of you, such preferences may only be a factor on weekends, because your day hours are set – you are in school.

   But if you are in college (or in a sixth form that mimics college's 'choose your own courses and times' timetabling), you would want to use this factor in determining when to arrange your lessons.

   If you study best in the morning, for example, try to schedule as many classes as possible in the afternoons (or, at worst, late in the morning). If you study best in the evening, either schedule morning classes and leave your afternoons free for other activities, or schedule them in the afternoons so you can sleep later (and study later the night before).

7 Some of us get irritable if we try to do anything when we are hungry. If you study poorly when your stomach is rumbling, eat something!

8 Most of us grow up automatically studying alone. If we study with a friend, there is often more horseplay than studying. But do not underestimate the positive effect studying with one or two friends – or even a larger study group – can have on your mastery of work and on your marks. (Study groups are discussed in greater detail at the end of this section.)

My Ideal Study Environment

How I receive information best:

1 ❑ Orally

   ❑ Visually

In the classroom, I should:

2 ❑ Concentrate on taking notes

   ❑ Concentrate on listening

3 ❑ Sit in front

   ❑ Sit at the back

   ❑ Sit near window or door

Where I study best:

4 ❑ At home

   ❑ In the library

   ❑ Somewhere else

   _____

When I study best:

5 ❑ Every night; little on weekends

   ❑ Mainly on weekends

   ❑ Spread out over seven days

6 ❑ In the morning

❑ Evening

❑ Afternoon

7 ❑ Before dinner

❑ After dinner

How I study best:

8 ❑ Alone

❑ With a friend

❑ In a group

9 ❑ Under time pressure

❑ Before I know I have to

10 ❑ With music

❑ In front of TV

❑ In a quiet room

11 ❑ Organising an entire night's studying before I start

❑ Tackling and completing one subject at a time

I need to take a break:

12 ❑ Every 30 minutes or so

❑ Every hour

❑ Every 2 hours

❑ Every _____ hours

9 Just because you perform best under pressure does not mean you should always leave projects, essays and studying for tests until the last minute. It shows if you are well organised, and if an unexpected project is assigned or a surprise test announced, you will not panic.

If you do not study well under pressure, it certainly does not mean you occasionally will not be required to do so. The better organised you are, the easier it will be for you all the time, but especially when the unexpected arises.

10 As we have discussed, some of you may find it difficult to concentrate without music or some sort of noise. Others could not sit in front of the TV and do anything but breathe and eat.

Many of you will fall in between – you can read and even take notes to music but need absolute quiet to study for a test or learn particularly difficult concepts. If you are not sure how you function best, now is the time to find out.

11 Back to organising. Starting and finishing one project before moving on to another does not mean you cannot at least sit down and outline an entire night's study plan before tackling each subject, one at a time. Setting up such a study plan is advised, but it may mean you really cannot move to another project while the one you are now working on is unfinished. Some of you may have no problem working on one project, switching to another when you get stuck or just need a break, then going back to the first.

12 There is nothing particularly wrong with taking a break whenever you feel you need to keep yourself sharp and maximise your quality study time… as long as the breaks are not every five minutes and do not last longer than the study periods. In general, though, try to increase your concentration through practice so that you can go at least an hour before getting up, stretching and having a cup of tea or snack. Too many projects will require at least that long to 'get into' or organise, and you may find that breaking too frequently will require too much 'review time' when you return to your desk.

Study groups: what are friends for?

Find a small group of like-minded students – four to six seems to be an optimal number – and share notes, question each other, prepare for tests together. To be effective, obviously, the students you pick to be in your study group should share all, or at least most, of your classes.

Search out students who are cleverer than you, but not too much. If they are on a level far beyond your own, you will soon be left behind and be more discouraged than ever. On the other hand, if you choose students who are too far beneath your level, you may enjoy being the 'brains' of the bunch but miss the point of the group – the challenge of other minds to spur you on.

Study groups can be organised in a variety of ways. Each member could be assigned primary responsibility for a single course, including preparing detailed notes from classes, lectures and discussion groups. If supplementary reading is recommended but not required, that person could be responsible for doing this and preparing detailed summaries.

Alternatively, everybody can be responsible for his or her own notes, but the group could act as an ad hoc discussion group, refining the understanding of key points, working on problems together, questioning each other, practising for tests, etc.

Even if you find only one or two other students willing to work with you, such cooperation will be invaluable, especially in preparing for major exams.

Tips for forming your own study group

▌ I suggest four students minimum, probably six maximum. You want to ensure everyone gets a chance to participate as much as they want while maximising the collective knowledge and wisdom of the group.

▌ While group members need not be best friends, they should not be overtly hostile to one another. Seek diversity of experience and demand common dedication.

▪ Try to select students who are at least as clever, committed and serious as you. That will encourage you to keep up and challenge you a bit. Avoid a group in which you are the 'star' – at least until you flicker out during the first exam.

▪ Avoid inviting members who are inherently unequal into the group, such as boyfriend/girlfriend combinations, in which one or the other may be inhibited by the other's presence; situations where one student works for another; situations where 'underdogs' (underachievers) and 'brainies' may stifle one another; etc.

▪ Decide early on if you are forming a study group or a social group. If the latter, do not pretend it is the former. If the former, do not just invite your friends and informally sit around discussing your teachers for an hour a week.

▪ There are a number of ways to organise, as we briefly discussed above. My suggestion is to assign each course to one student. That student must truly master that assigned course, doing, in addition to the regular assignments, of course, any or all additional reading (recommended by the tutor or not) necessary to achieve that goal, taking outstanding notes, outlining the course (if the group decides that would be helpful), being available for questions about specific topics in classes and preparing various practice tests, mid-terms and finals, as needed, to help test the other students' knowledge.

   Needless to say, all of the other students still attend all classes, take their own notes, do their own reading and homework assignments. But the student assigned that course attempts to learn as much as the tutor, to actually be the 'substitute lecturer' of that course in the study group. (So if you are taking five courses, a five-person study group becomes the ideal.)

▪ Make meeting times and assignments formal and rigorous. Consider establishing rigid rules of conduct. For example, miss two meetings, whatever the excuse, and you are out. Better to shake out the non-serious students early. You do not want anyone who is working as little as possible but hoping to take advantage of your hard work.

■ Consider appointing a chairperson (rotating, if you wish, weekly) in charge of keeping everyone to schedule and settling disputes before they disrupt the study group.

■ However you organise, clearly decide early the exact requirements and assignments of each student. Again, you never want the feeling to emerge that one or two of you are trying to 'jump on the bandwagon' of the others.

Where should you study?

■ **At the library.** There may be numerous choices, from the large reading room, to quieter, sometimes deserted speciality rooms, to your own study cubicle.

■ **At home.** Remember that this is the place where distractions are most likely to occur. No one tends to telephone you at the library and little brothers (or your own children) will not find you easily in there. But home is, of course, usually the most convenient place to make your study headquarters. It may not, however, be the most effective.

■ **At a friend's, neighbour's or relative's.** This may not be an option at all for most of you, even on an occasional basis, but you may want to set up one or two alternative study sites. Despite many experts' opinion that you must study in the same place every night (with which I don't agree), I have a friend who simply craves some variety to help motivate him. He has four different places he likes to study and simply rotates them from night to night. Do whatever works for you.

■ **In an empty classroom.** Certainly an option at many colleges and perhaps some independent schools, it is an interesting idea mainly because so few students have ever thought of it! While not a likely option at a state school, it never hurts to ask if you could make some arrangements. Since many athletic teams practise until 6pm or later, there may be a part of the school open – and usable with permission – even if the rest is locked up tight.

❙ **At your job.** Whether you are a student working part time or a full-timer going to college part time, you may be able to make arrangements to use an empty office, during regular office hours, or perhaps after everyone has left (depending on how much your boss trusts you). If you are in secondary school and a parent, friend or relative works nearby, you may be able to work from just after school until closing time at their workplace.

When should you study?

Try to create a routine time of day when you study. Some students find it easier to set aside specific blocks of time during the day, every day, in which they plan to study. The time of day you will study is determined by these factors.

1 **Study when you are at your best.** When is your peak performance period – the time of day you do your best work? This period varies from person to person – you may be dead to the world until noon but able to study well into the night, or up and alert at the crack of dawn but distracted and tired if you try to burn the midnight oil.

2 **Consider your sleep habits.** Habit is a very powerful influence. If you always set your alarm for 7am you may find that you wake up then even when you forget to set it. If you have become accustomed to going to sleep around 11pm you will undoubtedly become quite tired if you try to stay up studying until 2am, and probably accomplish very little in the three extra hours.

3 **Study when you can.** Although you want to sit down to study when you are mentally most alert, external factors also play a role in deciding when you study. Being at your best is a great goal but not always possible: study whenever circumstances allow.

4 **Consider the complexity of the assignment when you allocate time.** The tasks themselves may have a great effect on your schedule.

Evaluate your study area

Whatever location you choose as your study base, how you set up your study area can affect your ability to stay focused and, if you are not careful, seriously inhibit quality study time. Sit down at your desk or study area now and evaluate your own study environment.

1 Do you have one or two special places reserved just for studying? Or do you study wherever seems convenient or available at the time?

2 Is your study area a pleasant place? Would you offer it to a friend as a good place to study? Or do you dread it because it is so depressing?

3 How is the lighting? Is it too dim or too bright? Is the whole desk well lit? Or only portions of it?

4 Are all the materials you need handy?

5 What else do you do here? Do you eat? Sleep? Write letters? Read for pleasure? If you try to study in the same place you sit to listen to your music or chat on the phone, you may find yourself doing one when you think you are doing the other.

6 Is your study area in a high-traffic or low-traffic area? How often are you interrupted by people passing through?

7 Can you close the door to the room to avoid disturbances and outside noise?

8 When do you spend the most time here? At what time of day do you study? Is it when you are at your best, or do you inevitably study when you are tired and less productive?

9 Are your files, folders and other course materials organised and near the work area? Do you have some filing system in place for them?

Staying focused on your studies

If you find yourself doodling and dawdling more than read-ing and remembering, try the following solutions.

▌ **Create a work environment in which you are comfortable.** The size, style and placement of your desk, chair and light-ing may all affect whether or not you are distracted from the work at hand. Take the time to design the area that is perfect for you. Anything that you know will distract you – a girl-friend's picture, a radio or TV, whatever – should disappear from your study area.

▌ **Turn up the lights.** Experiment with the placement and in-tensity of lighting in your study area until you find what is best for you, both in terms of comfort and as a means of staying awake and focused.

▌ **Set some rules.** Let family, relatives and especially friends know how important your studying is and that specific hours are inviolate.

▌ **Take the breaks you need.** Do not just follow well-inten-tioned but bogus advice about how long you should study before taking a break. Break when you need to

Fighting tiredness and boredom

You have chosen the best study spot and no one could fault you on its set-up. You are still using matchsticks to prop up your eyelids? Help is on the way.

▌ **Take a nap.** What a thought. When you are too tired to study, take a short nap to revive yourself. Maximise that nap's effect by keeping it short – 20 minutes is ideal, 40 minutes absolute maximum. After that, you go into another phase of sleep and you may wake even more tired than before. If you cannot take such short naps now, train yourself to do so.

▪ **Have a drink.** A little caffeine will not harm you – a cup of coffee or tea, a glass of Cola. Just be careful not to overdo it – caffeine's 'wake-up' properties seem to reverse when you reach a certain level, making you far more tired than you were.

▪ **Turn down the heat.** Do not be cold, but too warm a room will inevitably make you doze... while your essay remains unwritten on your desk.

▪ **Shake a leg.** Go for a walk, jog around the kitchen, do a few step-ups – even mild physical exertion will give you an immediate lift.

▪ **Change your study schedule.** Presuming you have some choice here, find a way to study when you are normally more awake and/or most efficient.

Studying with small children

As many more of you are studying while bringing up a family, I want to give you some ideas that will help you cope with the Charge of the Preschool Light Brigade.

▪ **Plan activities to keep the children occupied.** The busier you are at college and/or at work, the more time your children will want to spend with you when you are at home. If you spend some time with them, it may be easier for them to play alone, especially if you have created projects they can work on while you are working on your homework.

▪ **Make the children part of your study routine.** Children love routine, so why not include them in yours? If 4–6pm is always 'Mum's Study Time', they will soon get used to it, especially if you make spending other time with them a priority and if you take the time to give them something to do during those hours. Explaining the importance of what you are doing – in a way that includes some ultimate benefit for them – will also motivate them to be part of your 'study team'.

▮ **Use the television as a baby-sitter.** While many of you will have a problem with this – it may be the lesser of two evils. You can certainly rent (or tape) enough quality films so you do not have to worry about the children watching street gangs bash skulls in (or bashing skulls themselves on some video game system).

▮ **Plan your study accordingly.** Unless you are a 'perfect parent', all these things will not keep your children from interrupting every now and then. While you can minimise such intrusions, it is virtually impossible to eliminate them entirely. So don't try – plan your schedule to include them. For starters, that means taking more frequent breaks to spend five minutes with your children. They will be more likely to give you the 15 or 20 minutes at a time you need if they get periodic attention themselves. By default, that means avoiding projects that can only be done with an hour of massive concentration – you can only work in 15 or 20 minute bursts.

▮ **Find help.** Spouses can occasionally take the children out for dinner and a film (the children will encourage you to study more if you institute this), relatives can baby-sit (at their homes) on a rotating basis, playmates can be invited over (allowing you to send your child to their house the next day), you may be able to swap baby-sitting chores with other parents at school and professional day care may be available at your child's school or in someone's home for a couple of hours a day.

Find out where you shine

It is the rare individual who is superior, or even good, in every subject. If you are, count your blessings. Most of us are a little better in one subject or another. Some of us simply like one subject more than another – and that changes your attitude towards it. Others are naturally gifted in one area, average in others.

For example, skill with numbers and spatial relations may come easily to you, but you may have absolutely no ear for music or languages. Or you may find learning a language a piece of cake, but not have the faintest clue why Pythagoras came up with his Theorem – or why you should care. Some students are good with their hands; others may find making the simplest item akin to torture.

Be thankful for whatever natural talents you possess and use the gift as a two-edged sword. Shift some study time from those tasks easily achieved to those that you find more difficult. The balance you will see in your development will be well worth the effort.

And if you have never really thought about the subjects you like and dislike, use the chart on page 45 to identify them. You will also be asked to identify those in which you perform well or poorly. (Teachers' reports on your work should confirm those.) Use this list to organise your own schedule to take advantage of your natural talents and give added time to subject areas that need the most work.

If you have a choice

All college students – and some secondary school students – are able to pick and choose courses according to their own schedules, likes, dislikes, goals, etc. The heartiness of such freedom should be tempered with the common-sense approach you are trying to develop through reading this book. Here are a few hints to help you along.

1 Whenever possible, consider each lecturer's reputation as you decide whether to select a particular course (especially if it is an overview or introductory course that is offered in two or three sections). Word soon gets around as to which lecturers' talks are stimulating and rewarding – an environment in which learning is a joy, even if it is not a subject you like.

2 Attempt to select lectures so your schedule is balanced on a weekly, and even daily, basis, although this will not always be possible or advisable. (Do not change your degree course just to fit your schedule.) Try to leave an open hour or half-hour between lectures – it is ideal for review, post-class note-taking, quick trips to the library and so on.

3 Try to alternate challenging classes with those that come more easily to you. Studying is a process of positive reinforcement. You will need encouragement along the way.

4 Avoid late-evening or early-morning classes, particularly if such scheduling provides you with large gaps of non-effective time.

5 Set a personal study pace and follow it. Place yourself on a study diet, the key rule of which is: do not overeat.

The landscape is littered with the shadows of unsuccessful students who have failed in their pursuits – not because they lacked the talent or motivation, but because they overloaded on information and pressure.

You can be successful without killing yourself!

Evaluation of Subject Areas

List the subject areas/courses you like most:

_____

_____

_____

_____

List those you like least:

_____

_____

_____

_____

List the courses in which you get the best marks:

_____

_____

_____

_____

And those in which you get the worst marks:

_____

_____

_____

_____

3 How to read and remember

Reading transforms and transports us through times past, present and future. Nothing you will do as you pursue your studies will be as valuable as the reading skills you develop – they are your ultimate long-term learning tool. Presuming you agree, what do you do?

Define your purpose for reading

What is your purpose in reading? If the best answer you can come up with is, 'Because my teacher said so' you need some better reasons. According to reading experts, there are six fundamental purposes for reading.

1 To grasp a certain message.

2 To find important details.

3 To answer a specific question.

4 To evaluate what you are reading.

5 To apply what you are reading.

6 To be entertained.

Using the clues in your textbooks

There are special sections found in nearly all textbooks and technical materials that contain a wealth of information and can help you glean more from your reading. Becoming familiar with this data will enrich your reading experience and often make it easier. This is what to look for.

The first page after the title page is usually the table of contents – a chapter-by-chapter list of the book's contents. Some are surprisingly detailed, listing every major point or topic covered in each chapter.

The first prose section (after the title page, table of contents and, perhaps, acknowledgements page, in which the author thanks other authors and his or her editor, typist, researcher, friends, relatives, teachers, etc – most of which can be ignored by the reader), the preface, is usually a description of what information you will find in the book. Authors may also use the preface to point out unique aspects of their books.

The introduction may be in place of or in addition to the preface and may be written by the author or some 'name' the author has recruited to lend additional prestige to his or her work. Most introductions are an even more detailed overview of the book – chapter-by-chapter summaries are often included to give the reader a feel for the material to be covered.

Footnotes may be found throughout the text (a slightly elevated number following a sentence, quote etc, eg, 'jim dandy'[24]) and either explained at the bottom of the page on which they appear or in a special section at the back of the text. Footnotes may be used to cite sources of direct quotes or ideas and/or to further explain a point, add information, etc, outside of the text. You may make a habit of finding sources cited in this way for further reading.

If a text tends to use an alarmingly high number of terms with which you may not be familiar, the considerate author will include a glossary – essentially an abridged dictionary that defines all these terms.

The bibliography, usually at the end of the book, may include the source material the author used to research the textbook, a list of 'recommended reading', or both. It is usually organised alphabetically by subject, making it easy for you to go to your library and find more information on a specific topic.

Appendices containing supplementary data or examples relating to subject matter covered in the text may also appear in the back of the book.

The last thing in a book is usually the index, an alphabetical listing that references, by page number, every mention of a particular name, subject, topic, etc in the text.

Making it a habit to utilise all of these tools in your textbooks can only make your studying easier.

Find other textbooks if necessary

While the authors and editors of most books might well be experts in a particular subject, writing in jargon-free, easy-to-grasp prose is probably not their strong point. You will occasionally be assigned a textbook that is so abstruse you are not even sure whether to read it front to back, upside down or inside out.

If you find a particular chapter, section or entire textbook tough to read go to the library or the bookshop and find another book covering the same subject area that you can understand.

If you do not grasp it, maybe it is because the author just does not know how to explain it. Perhaps it is not your fault. Too many students have sweated, moaned, dropped out of lessons, even changed degree courses because they thought they were dim, when it is possible that the textbook is useless, not you.

Use the clues in each chapter

Begin with a very quick overview of the assignment, looking for questions that you would like answered. Consider the following elements of your reading assignment before you begin your reading.

Chapter titles and bold-faced subheads announce the detail about the main topic. In some textbooks, paragraph headings or bold-faced 'lead-ins' announce that the author is about to provide finer details. So start each reading assignment by going through the chapter, beginning to end, reading only the bold-faced heads and subheads.

Look for end-of-chapter summaries. Knowing what the author is driving at in a textbook will help you look for the important building blocks for his conclusions while you are reading.

Most textbooks, particularly those in the sciences, will have charts, graphs, numerical tables, maps and other illustrations. Be sure to observe how they supplement the text and what points they emphasise, and make a note of these.

In some textbooks, you will discover that key terms and information are highlighted in italic or bold within the body text.

To find the definitions of these terms may then be your purpose for reading.

Some textbook publishers use a format in which key points are emphasised by questions, either within the body of or at the end of the chapter. If you read these questions before reading the chapter, you will have a better idea of what material you need to pay closer attention to.

If you begin your reading assignment by seeking out these heads, subheads and other purpose-finding elements of the chapter, you will have completed your prereading step. I advise that you always preread every assignment.

Three ways to read

Depending on what you are trying to accomplish in a particular reading assignment and the kind of book involved, there are three different ways to read. Knowing when to use each will make any assignment easier.

1 **Quick reference reading** focuses on seeking specific information that addresses a particular question or concern we might have.

2 **Critical reading** is used to discern ideas and concepts that require a thorough analysis.

3 **Aesthetic or pleasure reading** is for sheer entertainment or to appreciate an author's style and ability.

Skim first

Let me repeat this: the best way to begin any reading assignment is to skim the pages to get an overall view of what information is included. Then read the text carefully, word for word, and highlight the text and/or take notes in your notebook. (A brief digression: nearly everyone I know confuses 'skim' and 'scan'. Skim is to read quickly and superficially. Scan is to read carefully but for a specific item. So when you skim a reading passage, you are reading it in its entirety, though you are only grasping the 'highlights'. When you scan a passage, you are reading it in detail but only until you find what you are looking for. Scanning is the fastest reading rate of all – although you are reading in detail, you are not seeking to comprehend or remember anything that you see until you find the bit of information you are looking for.)

Newspapers make reading simple – gleaning the key news stories is as easy as reading the headlines and the first two or three paragraphs of each one.

Your textbooks are not always written to facilitate such an approach, but most of the authors probably make their key point of any paragraph in the first sentence of that paragraph. Succeeding sentences add the details. In addition, most of your textbooks include helpful marginal notes – those brief notes or headings in the outside margins of each page that summarise the topic covered in the paragraph or section. Or, like this book, include headings and subheadings to organise the material.

These standard organisational tools should make your reading job simpler. The next time you have to read a history, geography or similar text, try skimming the assigned pages first. Read the heads, the subheads and the marginal notes. Read the first sentence of each paragraph. Then go back and start reading the details.

By beginning your reading with a 20-minute skim of the text, you should be ready to answer three questions.

1 What is the text's principal message or viewpoint?

2 Is an obvious chain of thought or reasoning revealed?

3 What major points are addressed?

While the heads, subheads, first sentences and other author-provided hints we have talked about will help you get a quick read on what a chapter is about, some of the words in that chapter will help you concentrate on the important points and ignore the unimportant. Knowing when to speed up, slow down, ignore or really concentrate will help you read both faster and more effectively.

When you see words such as 'likewise', 'in addition', 'moreover' or 'furthermore', you should know nothing new is being introduced. If you already know what is going on, speed up or skip what is coming entirely.

On the other hand, when you see words like 'on the other hand', 'nevertheless', 'however', 'rather', 'but' and their ilk, slow down – you are getting information that adds a new perspective or contradicts what you have just read.

Lastly, watch out for 'pay-off' words such as 'in conclusion', 'therefore', 'thus', 'consequently', 'to summarise', especially if you only have time to 'grasp the high points' of a chapter or if you are reviewing for a test. This is where the real nub is. Slow down and pay attention.

Now go back for detail

If a more thorough reading is then required, turn back to the beginning. Read one section (chapter, etc) at a time.

As you read, make sure you know what is going on by asking yourself if the passage is written to address one of these questions.

1 **Who?** The paragraph focuses on a particular person or group of people. The topic sentence tells you who this is.

2 **When?** The paragraph is primarily concerned with time. The topic sentence may even begin with the word 'when'.

3 **Where?** The paragraph is oriented around a particular place or location. The topic sentence states where you are reading about.

4 **Why?** A paragraph that states reasons for some belief or happening usually addresses this question. The topic sentence answers why something is true or why an event happened.

5 **How?** A paragraph that identifies the way something works or the means by which something is done. The topic sentence explains the how or what is described.

Do not go on to the next chapter or section until you have completed the following exercise.

1 Write definitions of any key terms you feel are essential to understanding the topic.

2 Write questions and answers you feel clarify the topic.

3 Write any questions for which you do not have answers – then make sure you find them through rereading, further research or asking another student or your teacher.

4 Even if you still have unanswered questions, move on to the next section and complete points 1–3 above for that section. (And so on, until your reading assignment is complete.)

The challenge of technical texts

You have already learned a lot of ways to improve your reading. It is time to examine the unique challenges posed by highly technical texts – physics, trigonometry, chemistry, calculus – subjects that some of us try to avoid. More than any other kind of reading, these subjects demand a logical, organised approach, a step-by-step reading method. They also require a detection of the text's organisational devices.

Developing the skill to identify the basic sequence of the text will enable you to follow the progression of thought, a progression that is vital to your comprehension and retention.

In most technical writing, each concept is like a building block of understanding – if you do not understand a particular section or concept, you will not be able to understand the next section, either.

Most technical books are saturated with ideas, terms, formulas and theories. The chapters are dense with information, compressing a wealth of ideas into a small space. They demand to be read very carefully.

In order to get as much as possible from such reading assignments, you can take advantage of some devices to make sense of the organisation. Here are five basics to watch for.

1 Definitions and terms.

2 Examples.

3 Classifications and listings.

4 Use of contrast.

5 Cause–effect relationships.

In reading any specialised text, you must begin at the beginning – understanding the terms particular to that discipline. Familiar, everyday words have very precise definitions in technical writing. Everyday words can have a variety of meanings, some of them even contradictory, depending on the context in which they are used.

In contrast, in the sciences, terminology has fixed and specific meanings. For example, the definition of elasticity (the ability of a solid to regain its shape after a deforming force has been applied) is the same in Bangkok or Birmingham.

Another communication tool is the example. Technical writing is often filled with new or foreign ideas – many of which are not readily assimilated. They are difficult in part because they are abstract. Examples work to clarify these concepts, hopefully in terms more easily understood.

A third tool frequently utilised in texts is classification and listing. Classifying is the process by which common subjects are categorised under a general heading. Especially in technical writing, authors use classification to categorise extensive lists of detail. These writings may have several categories and subcategories that organise these details into some manageable fashion.

A fourth tool used in communicating difficult information is that of comparing and contrasting. Texts use this tool to bring complicated material into focus by offering a similar or opposing picture. Through comparison, a text relates a concept to one that has been previously defined – or to one a reader may readily understand. Through contrast, the text concentrates on the differences and distinctions between two ideas. By focusing on distinguishing features, these ideas become clearer as one idea is held up against another.

A final tool that texts employ to communicate is the cause–effect relationship. This device is best defined in the context of science, where it is the fundamental quest of most scientific research. Science begins with the observation of the effect – what is happening? It is snowing. The next step is to conduct research into the cause. Why is it snowing? Detailing this cause–effect relationship is often the essence of scientific and technical writing.

Read with a plan

More than any other type of writing, highly specialised, technical writing must be read with a plan.

Your plan should incorporate the following guidelines.

1 **Learn the terms** that are essential to understanding the concepts presented.

2 **Determine the structure of the text**. Most chapters have a pattern that forms the skeleton for the material. Often it can be discerned through the contents page or titles and subtitles.

3 **Skim the chapter** to get a sense of the author's viewpoint. Ask questions to define your purpose in reading. Use any summaries or review questions to guide your reading.

4 **Do a thorough analytical reading** of the text. Do not proceed from one section to the next until you have a clear understanding of the section you are reading – the concepts generally build upon each other.

5 **Immediately upon concluding your thorough reading, review**. Write a summary of the concepts and theories you need to remember. Answer any questions raised when you skimmed the text. Do the problems. If possible, apply the formulas.

Whether maths and science come easily to you there are some ways you can do better at such technical subjects.

▮ Whenever you can, 'translate' formulas and numbers into words. To test your understanding, try to put your translation into different words.

▮ Try translating a particularly difficult maths problem into a drawing or diagram.

▮ Before you even begin to solve a problem, try to estimate the answer.

▮ Play around. There are often different paths to the same solution, or even equally valid solutions. If you find one, try to find others.

▮ When you are checking your calculations, try working backwards.

▮ Try to work out what is being asked, what principles are involved, what information is important, what is not.

▮ Teach someone else. Trying to explain mathematical concepts to someone will quickly pinpoint what you really know or do not know.

Reading foreign language texts

Foreign language texts should be approached the same way, especially basic ones teaching vocabulary. If you have not mastered the words you are supposed to in the first section, you will have trouble reading the story at the end of section three, even if you have learned all the words in sections two and three. So take it one step at a time and make sure you have mastered one concept, vocabulary list, lesson, etc, before jumping ahead.

Aesthetic (pleasure) reading

*'To read a writer is for me not merely to get an idea of what he says,
but to go off with him, and travel in his company.'*
ANDRE GIDE

Most fiction is an attempt to tell a story. There is a beginning,
in which characters and setting are introduced. There is a conflict or struggle that advances the story to a climax where the
conflict is resolved. A final denouement unravels the conclusion of the story. Your literature class will address these parts
using terms that are often more confusing than helpful. The
following are brief definitions of some of the more important
ones.

Plot. The order or sequence of the story – how it proceeds from
opening through climax. Your ability to understand and appreciate literature depends upon how well you follow the plot
– the story.

Characterisation. The personalities or characters central to the
story – the heroes, the heroines and the villains. You will want
to identify the main characters of the story and their relationship to the struggle or conflict.

Theme. The controlling message or subject of the story, the
moral or idea that the author is using the plot and characters
to communicate.

Setting. The time and place in which the story occurs. This is
especially important when reading a historical novel or one
that takes you to another culture.

Point of view. Who is telling the story? Is it one of the central
characters giving you flashbacks or a first-person perspective?
Or is it a third-person narrator offering commentary and ob-
servations on the characters, the setting and the plot?

The first step in reading literature is to familiarise yourself with
these concepts, then try to recognise them in the novel or short

story. As you begin your reading, approach it first from an aesthetic standpoint. How does it make you feel? What do you think of the characters? Do you like them? Dislike them? Relate to them?

Second, make sure you know what is going on – this involves the plot or story-line and the development of the characters. On a chapter-by-chapter basis, you may find it helpful to keep a sheet of paper handy, on which you can write a sentence or two of the plot development (and, if you wish, characters introduced, etc).

How fast can you understand?

'When we read too fast or too slowly, we understand nothing.'
PASCAL

Are you worried that you read too slowly? You probably need not be – less rapid readers are not necessarily less able. What counts is what you comprehend and remember. Like anything else, practice will probably increase your speed levels. If you must have a ranking, read the 500-word passage below from start to finish. The section has been adapted from an American journal and discusses American politics. Note the elapsed time on your watch and score yourself as follows.

Under 30 seconds	very fast
31–45 seconds	fast
46–60 seconds	high average
61–89 seconds	average
90–119 seconds	slow
120 seconds or more	very slow

If you're like most members of the third estate, you wonder if there are any real differences between politicians who say they're liberal Democrats and those who say they are conservative Republicans. Aren't they all just slick-talking, vote-seeking, pocket-lining, power-hungry egomaniacs bent on getting elected? Maybe they are, but they also tend to have basic philosophical differences guiding their slick-talking, vote-seeking, pocket-lining, power-hungry pursuit of office.

Let's look at some fundamental political, social and economic differences between these groups.

Conservatives tend to champion free enterprise, or limited governmental control of the economy. They make the argument that people should be rewarded for their hard work and should not expect government handouts through the welfare system. They are also heavily into national defence, law enforcement and promotion of the fundamental values of family, God and country. (Makes you want to break out into several verses of 'The Star-Spangled Banner' doesn't it?)

Liberals take a more paternalistic view of government. It is the last and only hope for many members of society who have suffered at the unscrupulous or uncaring hands of others. They contend that business would run amok, exploiting workers and consumers in every market exchange, if not for government oversight. They also tend to be more concerned that everyone in society has equal access to a fair share of the economic pie, regardless of race, creed, sex, religion, shoe size, bank account, eye colour or planet of birth. Their hearts bleed for all.

These differences often place Republicans and Democrats on different sides of issues such as school prayer, environmental quality, welfare reform, worker safety, abortion, the death penalty, business regulation, sex education and, well, just about every other newsworthy topic over the past 10 gadzillion years.

Some of you might claim to be registered Democrats, yet you support school prayer and welfare reform, or contend you are Republican but sure as heck want clean air and water and are willing to fight for them. Does this make you schizophrenic or hypocritical? Not necessarily. In fact, there are few truly liberal Democrats or absolutely conservative Republicans who support the 'straight' party line. Many members of the third estate have a combination of liberal and conservative views... just like you.

Now answer the following questions without referring back to the text.

1 According to the author, which of the following do traditional Republicans not favour?

   A   School prayer
   B   Sex education
   C   Welfare reform
   D   Banning abortion

2 Republicans favour:

   A   Limited governmental control of the economy
   B   Free enterprise
   C   Both
   D   Neither

3 Democrats favour:

   A   Less stringent environmental laws
   B   Lower taxes
   C   Both
   D   Neither

4 The author is probably:

   A   A Democrat
   B   A Republican
   C   An independent
   D   A smart aleck

A good reader should be reading fast or very fast and have got at least three of the four questions correct. (Answers are at the end of the chapter.)

What decreases reading speed/comprehension?

1 Reading aloud or moving your lips when you read.

2 Reading mechanically – using your finger to follow words, and moving your head along as you read.

3 Applying the wrong kind of reading to the material.

4 Lacking sufficient vocabulary.

There are several things you can do to improve these reading mechanics.

To increase your reading speed

1 Focus your attention and concentration.

2 Eliminate outside distractions.

3 Provide for an uncluttered, comfortable environment.

4 Do not get stuck on single words or sentences, but do look up (in the dictionary) key words that you must understand in order to grasp an entire concept.

5 Try to grasp overall concepts rather than attempting to understand every detail.

6 If you find yourself moving your lips when you read (vocalisation), practise reading with a pen or some other (non-toxic, non-sugary) object in your mouth. If it falls out while you are reading, you know you have to keep working.

To increase comprehension

1 Try to make the act of learning sequential – comprehension is built by adding new knowledge to existing knowledge.

2 Review and rethink at designated points in your reading. Test yourself to see if the importance of the material is getting through.

3 If things do not add up, discard your conclusions. Go back, reread and try to find an alternative conclusion.

4 Summarise what you have read, rephrasing it in your notes and in your own words.

Most importantly, read at the speed that is comfortable for you. Though I can read extremely fast, I choose to read novels much more slowly so I can appreciate the author's word play. Similarly, any material that I find particularly difficult to grasp slows me down.

Should you take some sort of speed reading course, especially if your current speed level is slow? I cannot see that it could particularly hurt you in any way. I can also, however, recommend that you simply keep on practising reading, which will increase your speed naturally.

Remembering what you read

In a world where the ability to master and remember a growing explosion of data is critical for individual success, too little attention is paid to the dynamics of memory and systems for improving it. Developing your memory is probably the most effective way to increase your efficiency, in reading and virtually everything else.

There are some basic tools that will help you remember what you read.

- **Understanding**. You will remember only what you understand. When you read something and grasp the message, you have begun the process of retention.

- **Desire.** You remember what you choose to remember. To remember the material, you must want to remember it and be convinced that you will remember it.

- **Overlearn**. To really remember what you learn, you should learn material thoroughly, or overlearn. This involves pre-reading the text, doing a critical read and having some definite means of review that reinforces what you should have learned.

- **Systematise**. It is much more difficult to remember random thoughts or numbers than those organised in some pattern. For example, which phone number is easier to remember –

538-6284 or 678-1234? Have a system to help you recall how information is organised and connected.

▌ **Association**. Mentally link new material to existing knowledge so that you are giving this new thought some context in your mind.

Retention

Retention is the process by which we keep imprints of past experiences in our minds, the 'storage warehouse' and, depending on other actions of the mind, what is retained can be recalled when needed. Things are retained in the same order in which they are learned. So your studying should build one fact, one idea, one concept upon another.

Broad concepts can be retained more easily than details. Master generalities and details will fall into place.

If you think something is important, you will retain it more easily. So convincing yourself that what you are studying is something you must retain (and recall) increases your chances of adding it to your storehouse.

Retention is basically a product of what you understand. It has little to do with how fast you read, how good an outline you can construct or how many fluorescent colours you can highlight your textbooks with. Reading a text, grasping the message and remembering it are the fundamentals that make for high-level retention. Reading at a 1,000-word-per-minute rate does not necessarily mean that you have a clue as to what a text really says.

As you work towards improving your reading, realise that speed is secondary to comprehension. If you can read a passage of text faster than anyone in class, but cannot give a one-sentence synopsis of what you read, you lose. If you really grasp the author's message – even if it takes you an hour or two longer than some of your friends – your time will pay off in huge dividends now and in later life.

Recall

This is the process by which we are able to bring forth those things that we have retained. Recall can be strengthened through the process of repetition. Recall is least effective immediately after a first reading, emphasising the importance of review. The dynamics of our ability to recall are affected by several factors.

▮ We most easily recall those things that are of interest to us.

▮ Be selective in determining how much you need to recall. All information is not of equal importance – focus your attention on being able to recall the most important pieces of information.

▮ Allow yourself to react to what you are studying. Associating new information with what you already know will make it easier to recall.

▮ Repeat, out loud or just in your mind, what you want to remember. Find new ways of saying those things that you want to recall.

▮ Try to recall broad concepts as opposed to isolated facts.

▮ Use the new data you have managed to recall in a meaningful way – it will help you recall it the next time you need it.

Recognition

This is the ability to see new material and recognise it for what it is and what it means. Familiarity is the key aspect of recognition – you will feel that you have 'met' this information before, associate it with other data or circumstances and then recall the framework in which it logically fits.

If you have ever envied a friend's seemingly amazing ability to recall facts, dates and telephone numbers virtually at will, take heart that, in most cases, this skill is a result of study and practice, not something he was born with.

There are certain fundamental memory systems that, when grasped, can significantly expand your capability. It is beyond the scope of this book to teach you these detailed techniques, but if you feel you need help you will probably find a number of helpful titles in your local library as well as another book in this series, *Improve Your Memory*.

Why we forget

As you think about the elements of developing good memory, you can use them to work out why you forget. The root of poor memory is usually found in one of these areas.

1 We fail to make the material meaningful.

2 We did not learn the set texts.

3 We fail to grasp what is to be remembered.

4 We do not have the desire to remember.

5 We allow apathy or boredom to dictate how we learn.

6 We have no set habit for learning.

7 We are disorganised and inefficient in our use of study time.

8 We do not use the knowledge we have gained.

Build a library

> '*The reading of all good books is like conversation with the finest men of past centuries.*'
>
> DESCARTES

If you are ever to become an active, avid reader, access to books will do much to cultivate the habit. I suggest you 'build' your own library. Your selections can and should reflect your own tastes and interests, but try to make them wide and varied.

Include some of the classics, contemporary fiction, poetry and biography.

Save your school books – you will be amazed at how some of the material retains its relevance. Also try to read a good newspaper every day to keep up to date with current affairs.

Your local librarian can refer you to any number of lists of the 'classics', most of which are available in inexpensive paperback editions. Here are four more lists – compiled by myself – of the 'great' classical authors; the 'great' not-so-classical authors, poets and playwrights; some contemporary 'pretty goods' and a selection of 'good' works. You may want to put these on your 'to buy' list, especially if you are planning a summer reading programme.

I am sure that I have left off someone's favourite author or 'important' title from these lists. They are not meant to be comprehensive, just representative. I doubt anyone would disagree that a person familiar with the majority of authors and works listed here would be considered well read!

Some 'great' classical authors

Aeschylus	Cicero	S Johnson	Plato
Aesop	Confucius	Ben Jonson	Plutarch
Aquinas	Dante	Kant	Rousseau
Aristophanes	Descartes	Machiavelli	Shakespeare
Aristotle	Erasmus	Marx	Spinoza
Balzac	Flaubert	Milton	Virgil
Boccaccio	Goethe	Montaigne	Voltaire
J Caesar	Hegel	Nietzsche	
Cervantes	Homer	Ovid	
Chaucer	Horace	Pindar	

Some 'great' not-so-classical authors

W H Auden	Charlotte Brontë
Jane Austen	Emily Brontë
Samuel Beckett	Pearl Buck
William Blake	Lord Byron
Bertolt Brecht	Albert Camus

Lewis Carroll
Anton Chekov
Joseph Conrad
e e cummings
Daniel Defoe
Charles Dickens
Emily Dickinson
Fyodor Dostoevsky
Daphne du Maurier
Arthur Conan Doyle
Theodore Dreiser
Alexandre Dumas
George Eliot
T S Eliot
William Faulkner
F Scott Fitzgerald
E M Forster
Robert Frost
John Galsworthy
Jose Ortega y Gasset
Nikolai Gogol
William Golding
Maxim Gorky
Thomas Hardy
Nathaniel Hawthorne
Ernest Hemingway
Hermann Hesse
Victor Hugo
Aldous Huxley
Henrik Ibsen
Washington Irving
Henry James
James Joyce
Franz Kafka
John Keats
Rudyard Kipling
D H Lawrence
Harper Lee

Laurie Lee
C S Lewis
H W Longfellow
James Russell Lowell
Thomas Mann
W Somerset Maugham
Herman Melville
H L Mencken
Henry Miller
A A Milne
John Milton
H H Munro (Saki)
Vladimir Nabokov
O Henry
Eugene O'Neill
George Orwell
Dorothy Parker
Alan Paton
Boris Pasternak
Edgar Allan Poe
Ezra Pound
Marcel Proust
Ellery Queen
Erich Maria Remarque
Bertrand Russell
J D Salinger
George Sand
Carl Sandburg
William Saroyan
Jean-Paul Sartre
George Bernard Shaw
Percy Bysshe Shelley
Richard Brinsley Sheridan
Upton Sinclair
Alexander I Solzhenitsyn
Edmund Spenser
Gertrude Stein
John Steinbeck

Robert Louis Stevenson
August Strindberg
Jonathan Swift
Alfred Tennyson
Dylan Thomas
James Thurber
J R R Tolkien
Leo Tolstoy
Antony Trollope
Ivan Turgenev
Mark Twain
Robert Penn Warren

Evelyn Waugh
H G Wells
Walt Whitman
Oscar Wilde
Thornton Wilder
Tennessee Williams
P G Wodehouse
Thomas Wolfe
Virginia Woolf
William Wordsworth
William Butler Yeats
Emile Zola

Some 'pretty good' contemporary authors

Edward Albee
Kingsley Amis
Isaac Asimov
J G Ballard
John Barth
Saul Bellow
Anthony Burgess
A S Byatt
Truman Capote
John Cheever
Roald Dahl
Don DeLillo
E L Doctorow
Frederick Forsyth
John Fowles
Günter Grass
Nadine Gordimer
Grahame Greene
Joseph Heller
Lillian Hellman
Barry Hines
Thomas Keneally

Milan Kundera
John LeCarré
Norman Mailer
Bernard Malamud
Gabriel Garcia Marquez
Arthur Miller
Toni Morrison
Joyce Carol Oates
Flannery O'Connor
John Osborne
Joe Orton
Thomas Pynchon
Philip Roth
Salman Rushdie
Isaac Bashevis Singer
Tom Stoppard
David Storey
William Styron
John Updike
Kurt Vonnegut
Alice Walker
Eudora Welty

Some 'good' works

The Adventures of Huckleberry
   Finn
The Adventures of Tom Sawyer
The Aeneid
Aesop's Fables
Alice in Wonderland
All Quiet on the Western Front
Animal Farm
Anna Karenina
A Room with a View
As I Lay Dying
Babbitt
Beloved
The Bonfire of the Vanities
Brave New World
Brighton Rock
The Brothers Karamazov
Bury My Heart at Wounded Knee
The Canterbury Tales
Catch-22
The Catcher in The Rye
Cider with Rosie
A Clockwork Orange
The Color Purple
Confessions of an English
   Opium Eater
The Count of Monte Cristo
Crime and Punishment
Cry, the Beloved Country
David Copperfield
Death In Venice
Death of a Salesman
The Diary of Anne Frank
Don Juan
Don.Quixote
Dr Zhivago
Dr Jekyll and Mr Hyde
Ethan Fromme
Far From the Madding Crowd
A Farewell to Arms
The Fixer

For Whom the Bell Tolls
The French Lieutenant's Woman
The Good Earth
The Grapes of Wrath
The Great Gatsby
Gulliver's Travels
Hamlet
Heart of Darkness
Hedda Gabler
The Hitchhiker's Guide to the
   Galaxy
The Hobbit
The Hounds of the Baskervilles
Howard's End
I, Claudius
The Illiad
The Invisible Man
Jane Eyre
Jude the Obscure
Julius Caesar
Kim
King Lear
Lady Chatterley's Lover
A Lesson Before Dying
The Lion, the Witch and the
   Wardrobe
A Long Day's Journey Into Night
Look Back in Anger
Lord Jim
The Lord of the Flies
The Lord of the Rings
Lucky Jim
Macbeth
Man and Superman
The Merchant of Venice
The Metamorphosis
Midnight's Children
Moby Dick
Mother Courage
Native Son
1984

Of Human Bondage
Of Mice and Men
The Old Man and the Sea
Oliver Twist
One Day in the Life of Ivan Denisovich
One Flew Over the Cuckoo's Nest
One Hundred Years of Solitude
Othello
Our Town
The Outsider
Paradise Lost
A Passage to India
The Pickwick Papers
The Picture of Dorian Gray
A Portrait of the Artist as a Young Man
Portrait of a Lady
Possession
Pride and Prejudice
The Prophet
The Ragged-trousered Philanthropist
Ragtime
'The Raven'
Rebecca
The Red Badge of Courage
The Remembrance of Things Past
The Return of the Native
'The Road Not Taken'
Robinson Crusoe
Romeo and Juliet
The Scarlet Letter
Siddhartha

Silas Marner
Sister Carrie
Slaughterhouse 5
Sons and Lovers
Sophie's Choice
The Sound and the Fury
Steppenwolf
A Streetcar Named Desire
The Sun Also Rises
The Tale of Genji
A Tale of Two Cities
Tender is the Night
Tess of the d'Urbervilles
The Thin Red Line
This Sporting Life
The Time Machine
The Tin Drum
To Kill a Mockingbird
Tom Jones
To the Lighthouse
Treasure Island
The Trial
2001 – A Space Odyssey
Ulysses
Vanity Fair
Walden
War and Peace
'The Wasteland'
Watership Down
Wind in the Willows
Winne-The-Pooh
Wuthering Heights
Zen and the Art of Motorcycle Maintenance

Reading every one of these books will probably make you a better reader; it will certainly make you more well read. That is the extra added bonus to establishing such a reading programme – an appreciation of certain authors, certain books, certain cultural events and the like is what separates the cultured from the merely educated and the undereducated.

Read on

Insofar as one can in a single chapter, I have tried to sum up the essentials of reading. It is not a finite science, but rather a skill and appreciation that one can develop over time. Good basic education is essential. And for those of you who have been able to identify problem areas, there are always remedial classes. If you feel you need more help with your reading comprehension see also *Improve Your Reading* and *Improve Your Memory*, in this series.

Answers to quiz: B, C, D, D.

4 How to organise your time

We all have problems with time. We cannot control it – we cannot slow it down or speed it up. We cannot save it up – all we can do is decide how we are going to spend it. We invariably need more of it… and do not know where to find it. Then we wonder where it all went.

But time is not really the problem. After all, it is the one 'currency' that all people are given in equal supply, every day – 24 hours, the same for you, me and the Queen. The problem is that most of us simply let too much of it slip through our fingers – because we have never been taught how to manage our time… or why we should try. Our parents never sat us down to give us a little 'facts of time' talk, and time management skills are not part of any standard academic curriculum.

Whether you are a book author typing as fast as you can to meet a publisher's deadline, a student juggling five subjects and a part-time job or a parent working, attending classes and bringing up a family, a simple, easy-to-follow time management system is crucial to your success. And despite your natural inclination to proclaim that you just do not have the time to spend scheduling, listing and recording, it is also the best way to give yourself more time.

There may not be enough time for everything

When I asked one busy student if she wished she had more time, she joked, "I'm glad there are only 24 hours in a day. Any more and I wouldn't have an excuse for not getting everything done".

Let me give you the good news – there is a way that you can accomplish more in less time, one that is a lot more effective and does not take even more effort. You can plan ahead and make conscious choices about how your time will be spent, and how much time you will spend on each task. You can have more control over your time, rather than always running out of time as you keep trying to do everything.

Now the bad news – the first step to managing your time should be deciding just what is important… and what is not. Difficult as it may be, sometimes it is necessary for us to recognise that we really cannot do it all – to slice from our busy schedules those activities that are not as important to us so that we can devote more energy to those that are.

But there is enough time to plan

Yet, even after paring down our commitments, most of us are still challenged to get it all done. What with lectures or classes, study time, work obligations, extracurricular activities and social life, it is not easy fitting it all in.

The time management plan that I outline in this chapter is designed particularly for students. Whether you are in secondary school, college or university, a 'traditional student' or one who has chosen to return to education after being out in the 'real world' for a while, you will find that this is a manageable programme that will work for you.

The purpose of this chapter is to help you make choices about what is important to you, to help you set goals for yourself, to help you organise and plan your time and to develop the motivation and self-discipline to follow your schedule and reach those goals, which will give you the time to learn all the other study skills I write about.

Identify the starting line

Like any of the skills I have already talked about, you cannot race off to your ultimate goal until you work out where your starting line is. So the first step necessary to overhaul your current routine is to identify that routine, in detail. My suggestion is to chart, in 15-minute increments, how you spend every minute of every day. While a day or two might be sufficient for some of you, I recommend you chart your activities for an entire week, including the weekend.

This is especially important if, like many people, you have huge pockets of time that seem to disappear, but in reality are devoted to things like 'resting' after you wake up, putting on makeup or shaving, reading the paper, waiting for public transport or driving to and from school or work. Could you use an extra hour or two a day, either for studying or for fun? Make better use of such 'dead' time and you will find all the time you need.

For example, learn how to do multiple tasks at the same time. Listen to a book on tape while you are working around the house; practise vocabulary or maths tables while you are driving; ask your children, parents or roommates to test you for a forthcoming exam while you are washing up, vacuuming or dusting; and always carry your calendar, note-book(s), pens and a textbook with you – you can get a phenomenal amount of reading or studying done while queuing at the bank, in the library, at the supermarket or on a bus or train.

Strategy tip: Identify those items on your daily calendar, whatever their priority, that can be completed in 15 minutes or less. These are the ideal tasks to tackle at the launderette, while waiting for a librarian to locate a book you need or while queuing anywhere.

Collect what you need

As you begin your planning session, make sure you have all of the information and materials you need to make a quality plan. Gather your course syllabuses, work schedule, dates of important family events, holidays or trips, other personal commitments (doctor's appointments, parties) and a calendar of any extracurricular events in which you plan to participate.

Keeping track of your day-to-day activities (lessons, appointments, regular daily homework assignments and daily or weekly tests) will be dealt with after we talk about those projects – studying for mid-term exams and finals, termly assignments, theses – that require completion over a long period – weeks, maybe even months.

Creating your project board

There are two excellent tools you can use for your long-term planning. The first is a project board, which you can put on any blank wall or right above your desk. You can buy a ready-made chart at an art supply shop, stationer's or bookshop. Or you can copy the format of the one included on pages 76 and 77.

How does the project board work? As you can see, it is just a variation on a calendar. I have set it up vertically – the months running down the left-hand side, the projects across the top. You can change the order if you want. (Many shop-bought charts come set up in this way.)

Using your project board

For each project, there is a key preparatory step before you can use the chart: you have to break down each general assignment into its component parts. So, for example, for an English essay on Dante that has been assigned, I have identified the steps as:

1 Finalise topic.

2 Initial library research.

3 General outline.

4 Detailed library research.

5 Detailed outline.

6 First draft.

7 Second draft.

8 Check spelling and proofread.

9 Get someone else to proofread.

10 Type final draft.

11 Proofread again.

12 Hand it in.

Next to each specific task, I have estimated the time I would expect to spend on it. (For more information about the steps necessary to write a project assignment, see Chapter 8.)

The more time you have to complete a project, the easier it is to procrastinate dealing with it, even to put off identifying the steps and working them into your regular schedule. If you find yourself leaving long-term projects to the last week, schedule the projects furthest away – the termly assignment due in three months, the oral exam 10 weeks from now – first. Then trick yourself – schedule the completion date at least seven days prior to the actual handing in date, giving yourself a one-week cushion for life's inevitable surprises. (Then try to forget you have used this trick. Otherwise, you will be like the perennial latecomer who set his watch 15 minutes fast in an effort to get somewhere on time – except he always reminded himself to add 15 minutes to the time on his wrist, defeating the whole purpose.)

The other project involves working as a team with other students from your entrepreneurship course to create a hypothetical student business. While the steps are different, you will notice that the concept of breaking the project down into separate and manageable steps and allocating time for each does not change.

However, because time allocation in later steps depends on what assignments you are given by the group, we have had to temporarily place question marks next to some steps. As the details of this project become clearer and specific assignments are made, your project board should be changed to reflect both more details and specific time required for each step.

You should also include on your project board time for studying for all of your final exams. You have decided that every Sunday morning is 'review time' and allocated one Sunday a month to review the previous month's work in each subject.

Keep adding any other important projects throughout the term and continue to revise the board according to actual time spent as opposed to time allocated. Getting into this habit will make you more aware of how much time to allocate to future projects and make sure that the more you do so, the more accurate your estimates will be.

Sample Projects Board

MONTH/WEEK		PROJECT: STUDENT CORPORATION
1st MONTH	Week 1	Initial group meeting: discuss overall assignment and possible products or services – bring list of three each to meeting (1 hour)
	Week 2	Finalise product or service; finalise organisation of group and long-term responsibilities of each subgroup (3)
	Week 3	Subgroup planning and short-term assignments (2)
	Week 4	Work on individual assignment from subgroup (?)
2nd MONTH	Week 1	Work on individual assignment from subgroup (?)
	Week 2	Work on individual assignment from subgroup (?)
	Week 3	Integrate individual assignment with rest of subgroup (?)
	Week 4	Meet with entire group to integrate plans (?)
3rd MONTH	Week 1	Finalise all-group plan; draft initial report (?)
	Week 2	Type and proof final report (?)
	Week 3	
	Week 4	
	DUE DATE	3rd Month/end of Week 2

PROJECT: DANTE TERM ESSAY	REVIEW/EXAM SCHEDULE
Finalise topic (1 hour)	Review prior month's history notes (3)
Initial library research (2)	Review prior month's English notes (2)
Detailed library research (3)	Review prior month's science notes (4)
Detailed library research (3)	Review prior month's maths notes (4)
Detailed library research (3)	Review 1st Month history notes (3)
Detailed outline (1)	Review 1st Month English notes (2)
First draft (4), Additional research (2)	Review 1st Month science notes (4)
	Review 1st Month maths notes (4)
Second draft, spellcheck, proof (10)	2nd Month history notes (3)
Independent proof (1)	2nd Month English notes (2)
	2nd Month science notes (4)
Type final draft and proof (4)	2nd Month maths notes (4)
End of 3rd Month	End of 3rd Month

Using a term planning calendar

The term planning calendar should be used together with the project board. A blank example form that you could adapt for your own use is on page 85.

Start by transferring all the information from the project board to your term planning calendar. Then add your weekly lesson schedule, work schedule, family celebrations, holidays and trips, club meetings and extracurricular activities – everything. The idea is to make sure your calendar has all the scheduling information, while your project board contains just the briefest summary that you can take in at a glance.

Leave your project board on your wall at home; carry your term calendar with you. Whenever new projects, appointments or meetings are scheduled, add them immediately to your calendar. Then transfer the steps involving major projects to your project board.

Secondary school students may find it quite easy to use only the calendar, as they are usually not subject to quite as many long-term projects as college or university students. But once you are in college, especially if you have more than an average number of essays, reports, projects, etc, you will find the project board a very helpful extra tool.

Planning your days and weeks

For any time management system to work, it has to be used continually. Make an appointment with yourself at the end of each week – Sunday night is perfect – to sit down and plan for the following week. This may be the best time you spend all week, because you will reap the benefits of it throughout the week and beyond.

Step 1: Make a 'to-do' list

First, you must identify everything you need to do this week. Look at your project board and/or term calendar to determine what tasks need to be completed this week for all your major college projects. Add any other tasks that must be done this week: from sending off a birthday present to your sister to attending your monthly volunteer meeting to completing homework that may have recently been assigned.

Step 2: Prioritise your tasks

When you sit down to study without a plan, you just dive into the first project that comes to mind. Of course there is no guarantee that the first thing that comes to mind will be the most important. The point of the weekly priority task sheet is to help you arrange your tasks in order of importance. That way, even if you find yourself without enough time for everything, you can at least finish those assignments that are most important. A blank form is given as an example on page 86.

First, ask yourself this question, 'If I only got a few things done this week, what would I want them to be?' Mark these high-priority tasks with an 'H.' After you have identified the 'urgent' items, consider those tasks that are least important – items that could wait until the following week to be done, if necessary. You may have tasks that you consider very important, but that do not have to be completed this week. These items might be less important this week, but are likely to be rated higher next week. These are low-priority items; mark them with an 'L.'

Strategy tip: If you push aside the same low-priority item day after day, week after week, at some point you should just stop and decide whether it is something you need to do at all. This is a strategic way to make a task or problem 'disappear'. In the business world, some managers purposefully avoid confronting a number of problems, waiting to see which will simply solve themselves through benign neglect. If it works in business, it can work for you in school.

All other responsibilities fit somewhere between the critical tasks and those of low priority. Review the remaining items, and if you are sure that none of them are either 'H' or 'L', mark them with an 'M' (to represent middle priority).

Step 3: Fill in your daily schedule

Before you start adding essays, projects, homework, study time, etc, to your calendar, fill in the 'knowns' – the time you need to sleep, eat, work, attend class. Even if your current routine consists of meals on the run and sleep wherever you find it, build the assumption into your schedule that you are going to get eight hours of sleep and three decent meals a day. You may surprise yourself and find that there is still enough time to do everything you need. (Although all of us probably know someone who sleeps three hours a night, eats only junk and still finds a way to get nothing but As, most experts would argue that regular, healthy eating and a decent sleep schedule are key attributes of any successful study system.)

Now transfer the items on your priority task sheet to your daily schedule forms. (See page 87 for an example blank form.) Put in the 'H' items first, followed by the 'M' items. Then, fit in as many of the 'L' items for which you still have room.

By following this procedure, you will ensure you give the amount of time needed to your most important priorities. You can devote your most productive study times to your most important tasks, and slot in your lower priorities as they fit.

Besides the importance of the task and the available time you have to complete it, other factors will determine how you fit your daily schedules together. Some will be beyond your control: work schedules, appointments with lecturers, doctors, etc. But there are plenty of factors you do control, which you should consider as you put together your daily schedules for the week.

Do not overdo it. Plan your study time in blocks, breaking up work time with short leisure activities. It is helpful to add these to your schedule as well. You will find that these breaks help you think more clearly and creatively when you get back to studying.

Even if you tend to like longer blocks of study time, be careful about scheduling study 'marathons' – six- or eight-hour stretches rather than a series of two-hour sessions. The longer the period you schedule, the more likely you will have to fight against procrastination. By convincing yourself that you are really studying your heart out, you will also find it easier to justify time-wasting distractions, putting in longer breaks and, before long, giving up before you should.

Make sure you use your daily schedule *daily*. That is what it's there for. Each night (or when you wake up in the morning) look at your schedule for the forthcoming day. How much free time is there? Are there 'surprise' tasks that are not on your schedule but need to be? Are there conflicts you were not aware of at the beginning of the week? By checking your daily schedule daily, you will be able to respond to these changes.

Strategy tip: Get into the habit of getting ready for the next day before you go to bed the night before. It is an absolutely fantastic feeling to start the day completely organised... especially if you oversleep.

Using these tools effectively

There are thinkers and there are doers.

Then there are those who think a lot about doing.

Organising your life requires you to actually use the project board, term planning calendar, priority task sheets and daily schedules. Once you have discovered habits and patterns of study that work for you, continue to use and polish them. Be flexible enough to add techniques you learn from others and alter schedules that circumstances have made obsolete.

Plan according to your schedule, your goals and your aptitudes, not some ephemeral 'standard'. Allocate the time you expect a project to take you, not the time it might take someone else, or how long your teacher says it should take, etc. Try to be realistic and honest with yourself when determining those things that require more effort or those that come easier to you.

Whenever possible, schedule pleasurable activities after study time, not before. They will then act as incentives, not distractions.

Monitor your progress at reasonable periods and make changes where necessary. This is your study regime – you conceived it, you can change it. If you find that you are consistently allotting more time than necessary to a specific chore, change your future schedule accordingly.

As assignments are entered on your calendar, make sure you also enter items needed – texts, other books you have to buy, borrow or get from the library and materials such as drawing pads, magic markers, graph paper, etc.

You may decide that colour coding your calendar – red for assignments that must be accomplished that week, blue for steps in longer-term assignments, yellow for personal time and appointments, green for lectures, etc – makes it easier for you to tell at a glance what you need to do and when you need to do it.

Adapt these tools for your own use. Try anything you think may work – use it if it does, discard it if it does not.

Do your least favourite chores (study assignments, projects, whatever) first – you will feel better having got them out of the way. Plan how to accomplish them as meticulously as possible. That will get rid of them even faster.

Accomplish one task before going on to the next one – do not skip around.

If you see that you are moving along faster than you anticipated on one task or project sequence, there is absolutely nothing wrong with continuing on to the next part of that assignment or the next project step.

If you are behind, do not panic. Just reorganise your schedule and find the time you need to make up.

Write things down. Not having to remember all these items will free up space in your brain for the things you need to concentrate on or do have to remember.

Learn to manage distractions. As a time management axiom puts it, 'Don't respond to the urgent and forget the important'. Some things you do can be picked up or dropped at any time. Beware of those time-consuming and complicated tasks that, once begun, demand to be completed. Interrupting at any point might mean starting all over again. What a waste of time that would be.

If you are writing and you have a brainstorm just as the phone rings (and you know the call is from that person you have been waiting to hear from all week), take a minute to at least jot down your ideas before you stop.

Nothing can be as counterproductive as losing your concentration, especially at critical times. Learn to ward off those enemies that would alter your course and you will find your journey much smoother.

One way to guard against these mental intrusions is to know your own study clock and plan accordingly. Each of us is predisposed to function most efficiently at specific times of day (or night). Find out what sort of study clock you are on and schedule your work during this period.

Beware of uninvited guests and all phone calls – unless you are ready for a break, they will only get you off schedule. More subtle enemies include the sudden desire to sharpen every pencil in the house, an unheard-of urge to clean your room, an offer to do your sister's homework. Anything to avoid your own work. If you find yourself doing anything but your work, either take a break then and there, or pull yourself together and get down to work. Self-discipline, too, is a learned habit that gets easier with practice.

The simple act of saying no (to others or to yourself) will help insulate you from these unnecessary (and postponable) interruptions. Remember, what you are seeking to achieve is not just time – but quality time. Put your 'Do not disturb' sign up and stick to your guns, no matter what the temptation.

Remember that time is relative. Car trips take longer if you have to schedule frequent stops for fuel, food, necessities, etc, longer still if you start out during rush hour. Similarly, libraries are more crowded at certain times of the day or year, which will affect how fast you can get books you need, etc. So take the time of day into account.

And if your schedule involves working with others, you need to take their sense of time into account – you may find you have to schedule 'waiting time' for a chronically late friend… and always take a book along.

A special note for commuters

If you live at home (as opposed to being housed on campus), there are some special pressures with which you need to contend.

Travelling to college will probably be longer than if you could roll out of bed and walk there. It will require more wakefulness, even if you only have to stumble to a station or bus (but especially if you have to drive). You will also have travel time problems if you need to return to the campus for any reason after you have returned home. It is especially important that you minimise travel time, planning enough to maximise your use of the campus facilities without scheduling a trip home in between.

While nobody likes walking in rain, sleet or snow – except, perhaps, postal employees – it is invariably easier to walk a few tree-lined streets than drive a few miles in inclement weather. Take weather problems into account when planning your journey.

The very act of living at home – whether as a child or one 'married with children' – brings with it responsibilities to others you could minimise by living-in at college. Be ready to allocate time to these responsibilities and include them in your study schedule. They are an inevitable part of life if you live at home.

Now comes the payoff

Once you start using your project board, term planning calendar, priority task sheets and daily schedules, you will reap the benefits every day.

Anything – even learning – seems less overwhelming when you have it broken into 'bite-size' pieces… and you already know the flavour.

You no longer worry about when you will get that essay written – you have already planned the time.

You will accomplish it all – one step at a time.

My time management programme allows for flexibility and I encourage you to adapt any of my recommendations to your own unique needs. That means it will work for you whether you are living in a college, sharing an apartment or house with roommates or living with a partner and children. You can learn how to balance college, work, fun and even family obligations.

As you get used to managing your time, planning well ahead as well as planning your week and even your days, you will quickly discover that you seem to have more time than ever before.

(The forms on pages 85–7 can be adapted for your own time management system.)

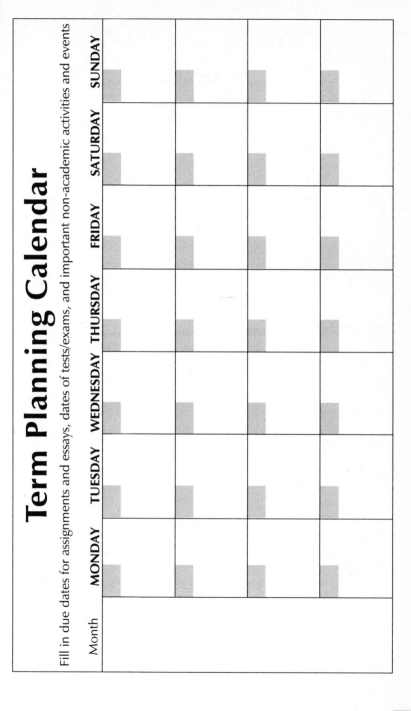

Term Planning Calendar

Fill in due dates for assignments and essays, dates of tests/exams, and important non-academic activities and events

Month	MONDAY	TUESDAY	WEDNESDAY	THURSDAY	FRIDAY	SATURDAY	SUNDAY

Priority rating	Scheduled?	**Priority Tasks This Week**
		Week beginning ▭ and ending ▭

Daily Schedule

date:

Assignments Due

| |
| |
| |
| |
| |

To Do/Errands

| |
| |
| |
| |
| |
| |
| |
| |

Homework

| |
| |
| |
| |
| |
| |

Schedule

| 5 |
| 6 |
| 7 |
| 8 |
| 9 |
| 10 |
| 11 |
| 12 |
| 1 |
| 2 |
| 3 |
| 4 |
| 5 |
| 6 |
| 7 |
| 8 |
| 9 |
| 10 |
| 11 |
| 12 |

5 How to excel in the classroom

Whatever your grade level, whatever your marks, whatever your chosen course, whatever your ultimate career goal, we all have one thing in common: the classroom experience.

Most teachers use the classroom setting as an opportunity to embellish and interpret material covered in the text and other assigned readings. If you always complete your reading assignments before the lesson or seminar, you will be able to devote your classroom time to the 'add-on' angles the teacher will undoubtedly cover.

You have got to have class

Exactly how you use the skills covered in this chapter will be influenced by two factors: the type of classroom set-up and the particular methods and styles employed by each of your teachers.

Each of the following general classroom formats will require you to make adjustments to accomplish your goals.

Lectures: podium pleasantries

Teacher speaks, students listen. Pure lectures are quite common from the college level up, but exist only rarely at secondary school level. Lecture halls at larger colleges and universities may fill up with hundreds of students for some of the more popular courses.

Primary emphases: listening; note-taking.

Discussions: time to speak your mind

Also called tutorials and seminars, discussion groups are again common at the college and university level, often as adjuncts to courses boasting particularly large enrolments. A typical weekly schedule for such a course might consist of two lectures and one or more discussion groups or tutorials. These discussion groups contain fewer students – usually no more than two dozen – and give you the chance to discuss points made in the lecture and material from assigned readings.

Such groups rarely follow a precise text or format and may wander wildly from topic to topic, once again pointing out the need for a general mastery of the course material, the 'jumping off' point for discussion.

Primary emphases: asking/answering questions; analysing concepts and ideas; taking part in discussion.

Combination: best (or worst) of both

Some university courses are, for want of a better term, combination classes; they combine the lecture and discussion formats. The teacher prepares a lecture plan of material he or she wants covered in a specific course. Through lecture, discussion, question and answer, audio-visual presentation or a combination of one or more such devices, the material is covered. Your preparation for this type of lesson will depend to a great extent on the approach of each individual lecturer. Such lessons also occur on the sixth form college level – college, apprenticeship courses, evening classes – when class size is too small for a formal lecture approach.

Primary emphases: note-taking; listening; participation, asking and answering questions.

Hands-on: getting your hands dirty

Classes such as science labs and various vocational education courses (industrial arts, graphics, etc), occur at all levels from secondary school upwards. They are concerned almost exclusively with doing something – completing a particular experiment, working on a project, etc. The teacher may demonstrate certain things before letting the students work on their own, but the primary emphasis is on the student carrying out his or her own projects while in the classroom.

At university level, science labs may be overseen by postgraduate assistants. Apprenticeship courses may use a combination of short lectures, demonstrations and hands-on workshops; you cannot become a good car mechanic just by reading a book on how to clean a distributor.

Primary emphasis: development and application of particular manual and technical skills.

Exceptions to the rule

Rarely can a single course be neatly pigeonholed into one of these formats, though virtually all will be primarily one or another. It would seem that size is a key factor in choosing a format, but you cannot always assume, for example, that a large lecture course, filled with 200 or more students, will feature a lecturer standing behind a rostrum reading from his prepared text. Or that a small group of a dozen people will tend to be all discussion in a tutorial or seminar format.

During my college years, I had a religion teacher who, though his course was one of the more popular and regularly drew 300 or more students to each session, rarely lectured at all. I never knew what to expect when entering his classroom. One week it would be a series of musical improvisations from a local jazz band, with a variety of postgraduate assistants talking about out-of-body (religious, note the tie-in) experiences. Another session would consist entirely of the professor arguing with a single student over one key topic... which had nothing to do with that week's (or any other week's) assignment.

On another course of merely 20 students, the professor teaching us physical chemistry would march in at the sound of the bell and, without acknowledging anyone's presence or saying a word, walk to the blackboard and start writing equations, which he would continue to do, working his way across the massive board, until, some 20 or 30 minutes later, he ran off the right side. Slowly, he would walk back to the left side... and start writing all over again. He never asked questions. Never asked for questions. In fact, I am not sure I remember him uttering anything for three solid months.

Know your teacher

What is also extremely important for you to know and understand is the kind of teacher you have and his or her likes, dislikes, preferences, style and what he or she expects you to get out of his or her lesson. Depending on your analysis of your teacher's habits, goals and tendencies, preparation may vary quite a bit, whatever the chosen format.

Some teachers are very confident fielding questions at any point during a lesson; others prefer questions to be held until the end of the lesson; still others (my chemistry professor is a good example) discourage questions (or any interaction for that matter) entirely. Learn when and how your teacher likes to answer questions and ask accordingly.

No matter how ready a tutorial group is to enter into a free-wheeling discussion, some teachers fear losing control and veering away from their very specific lesson plan. These teachers may well encourage discussion but always try to steer it into the set path they have decided upon. Other teachers thrive on chaos, in which case you can never be sure just what is going to happen.

Approaching a lesson with the former teacher should lead you to participate as much as possible in the classroom discussion, but warn you to stay within whatever boundaries he or she has obviously set.

Getting ready for a lesson taught by the latter kind of teacher requires much more than just reading the text – there will be a lot of emphasis on your understanding key concepts, interpretation, analysis and your ability to apply those lessons to cases never mentioned in your text at all.

Some teachers' lesson plans or lectures are, at worst, a review of what is in the text and, at best, a review plus some discussion of tricky points or areas he or she feels may give you problems. Others use the text or other assignments merely as a jumping-off point – their lectures or lesson plans might cover numerous points that are not in your text at all. Preparing for the latter will require much more than rote memorisation of facts and figures – you will have to be ready to give examples, explain concepts in context and more.

Most of your teachers and professors will probably have the same goals: to teach you how to think, learn important facts and principles of the specific subject they teach and, perhaps, how to apply them in your own way.

In lessons like maths or science, your ability to apply what you have learned to specific problems is paramount. Others, like English, will require you to analyse and interpret various works, but may emphasise the 'correct' interpretation, too.

Whatever situation you find yourself in – and you may well have one or more of each of the above 'types' – you will need to adapt the skills we will cover in this chapter to each situation.

How to prepare for any lesson

In general, here is how you should plan to prepare for any lesson before you walk through the door and take your seat.

Complete all assignments

Regardless of a particular teacher's style or the classroom format he or she is using, virtually every course you take will have a formal text (or several) assigned to it. Although the way the text explains or covers particular topics may differ substantially from your teacher's approach to the same material, your text is still the basis of the course and a key ingredient in your studying. You must read it, plus any other assigned books, before arriving at the lesson.

You may sometimes feel you can get away without reading assigned books beforehand, especially in a lecture format where you know the chance of being called on is fairly slim. But fear of being questioned on the material is certainly not the only reason I stress reading the material that has been assigned. You will be lost if the lecturer decides – for the first time ever – to spend the entire period asking the students questions. I have experienced this and it is not pleasant for the unprepared.

You will also find it harder to take clear and concise notes because you will not know what is in the text (and you will be frantically taking notes on material you could have underlined or highlighted in your books the night before, if you had read them, of course) or be able to evaluate important versus unimportant information.

If you are going to a discussion group, how can you participate without reading the text as a basis? I think one of the worst feelings in the world is sitting in a classroom knowing that, sooner or later, you are going to be called on and you do not know the material.

Remember: this includes not just reading the main text but any other books, articles, handouts, etc, previously assigned. It also means completing any non-reading assignments – handing in a lab report, preparing a list of topics, being ready to present your oral report, etc.

Review your notes

Both from your reading and from the previous lecture. Your teacher is probably going to start this lecture or discussion from the point he or she left off last time and you probably will not remember where that point was, unless you check your notes.

Have questions ready

As I discussed in Chapter 3, preparing questions as you read text material is an important step. This is your chance to find the answers to the questions that are still puzzling you. Review your questions before the lecture so you will be able to tick off the ones the lecturer or teacher answers along the way and you will only need to ask those left unanswered.

Prepare required materials

Include your notebook, text, pens or pencils and other such basics, plus any particular lecture requirements like a calculator, drawing paper, other books, etc.

Before we get into how to take notes, it is important to talk about how to set up your notebook(s). There are a variety of ways you can organise your note-taking system.

1 **Get one big ring binder** (probably three or more inches thick) that will be used for all notes from all your courses. This will require a hole punch, tabbed card dividers and a good supply of pre-punched paper.

You can divide the binder into separate sections for each course/class, in each of which you will keep notes from your lectures and discussion groups, reading lists, assignment deadlines and any course handouts – all material set up in chronological fashion. Alternatively, you can further subdivide each section into separate sections for reading notes, lesson notes and handouts.

This system has two key disadvantages:

(a) Holes that constantly tear, requiring you to patiently paste on those reinforcing circles, a boring and time-wasting task;

(b) Woe unto ye who lose your binders, for within them is everything ye cherish, and surely ye shall wallow in a sea of incompleteness.

The former problem can be solved by using either a spring-operated binding mechanism – which requires no holes at all, let alone 'reinforcements' – or a multi-pocket file folder in which weekly or daily notes can be stapled together and filed along with handouts, assignments, etc.

The latter problem can be solved by selectively 'culling' your notebook every week (perhaps at the same time as you plan the next week) so, at worst, you lose a week's worth of material, not an entire term's.

2 **Use one of the above systems but get smaller binders** – for each course/class (with the same options regarding the type of binder and how to protect yourself from losing all your notes – if only from a single course).

3 **Use separate notebooks** (they are a lot lighter than binders) for notes, both from your reading and lesson. Use file folders for each course to keep handouts, project notes and copies, etc. They can be kept in an accordion file or in a multi-pocketed folder.

Whichever system you choose – one of the above or an ingenious one of your own – do not use the note card system for preparing assignments and oral reports you will learn in

Chapter 8. While it is my all-time favourite system for that application, it does not work well for lecture note-taking... and I have tried it.

Prepare your attitude

Do not discount the importance of the way you approach each lesson mentally. Getting the most out of school or college in general and any lesson in particular depends in good measure on how ready you are to really take part in the process. You must be 'able and willing' for school, 'able and willing' for each lesson. It is not sufficient, even if you are otherwise well prepared, to just sit back and absorb the information. Learning requires your active participation every step of the way.

What to do in the classroom

Keep in mind your own preferences and under what circumstances you do best – refer back to the first two chapters and review your skills lists. You will need to concentrate hardest on those courses in which you do most poorly, no matter what the style of the teacher.

Sit near the front

Reduce distraction as much as possible by sitting as close to the teacher as you can.

You have probably realised by now that the farther you sit from the teacher, the more difficult it is to listen. Sitting towards the back of the room means more heads bobbing around in front of you and more students staring out the window... and encouraging you to do the same.

Sitting at the front has several benefits. You will make a good impression on the teacher since you might be the only student in the front row. He will see immediately that you have come to the lesson to listen and learn, not just to take up space. You will be able to hear the teacher's voice clearly, and in turn he will be able to hear you clearly.

Finally, being able to see the teacher clearly will help ensure that your eyes do not wander around the room and out of the window, taking your brain with them. If you have the option of picking your seat, go straight to the front of the classroom.

Avoid distracting classmates

The crisp eater. The doodler. The practical joker. The whisper-er. Even the perfume sprayer. Your fellow classmates may be kind and thoughtful friends, entertaining lunch companions and great fun at parties, but their little quirks, idiosyncrasies and personal hygiene habits can prove distracting when you sit next to them in the classroom. Knuckle-cracking and note-passing are just some of the evils that can divert your attention in the middle of your biology teacher's discourse on bivalves. Avoid them.

Sit up straight

Do I sound like your parents? I know you do not want to hear it, but for once they are right. To listen effectively, you must sit in such a way that will let you stay comfortable and relatively still during the entire lecture. If parts of your body start to ache or fall asleep, your attention will inevitably wander. Remember: 'The mind can retain only as much as the bottom can sustain'.

Listen for verbal clues

Identifying noteworthy material means separating the wheat – that which you should write down – from the chaff – that which you should ignore. Do that by listening for verbal clues and watching for nonverbal ones.

Certainly not all teachers will give you the clues you are seeking. However, many will invariably signal important material in the way they present it – pausing (waiting for all the pens to rise), repeating the same point (perhaps even one already made and repeated in your textbook), slowing down their normally supersonic lecture speed, speaking more loudly (or more softly), even simply stating, 'I think the following is important'.

There are also a number of words that should signal noteworthy material (and, simultaneously, give you the clues you need to logically organise your notes): 'first of all', 'most importantly', 'therefore', 'as a result', 'to summarise', 'on the other hand', 'on the contrary', 'the following (number of) reasons (causes, effects, decisions, facts, etc)'.

These (and similar words and phrases I am sure you can think of) give you the clues to not only write down the material that follows, but to put it in context – to make a list ('first', 'the following reasons'); establish a cause-and-effect relationship ('therefore', 'as a result'); establish opposites or alternatives ('on the other hand', 'on the contrary'); signify a conclusion ('therefore', 'to summarise'); or offer an explanation or definition.

Watch for nonverbal clues

Studies have shown that only a fraction of communication is carried in words themselves. A great deal of the message we receive when someone is speaking to us comes from body language, facial expression and tone of voice.

Most teachers will go off on tangents of varying relevance to the subject matter. Some of these will be important, but, at least during your first few lessons with that particular teacher, you will not know which.

Body language can be the clue. If the teacher is looking at the window or his eyes glaze over, he is sending a clear signal: 'This will not be on any test'.

On the other hand, if he turns to write something down on the blackboard, makes eye contact with several students and/ or gestures dramatically, he is sending a very obvious signal about the importance of the point he is making.

Of course, there are exceptions to this rule. There was a trigonometry professor I endured who would get most worked up about the damage being done to the nation's pavements by the deadly menace of chewing gum.

Teachers like to see students taking notes. It shows you are interested in the topic and that you think enough of what is being said to write it down. (Also, if you have ever stood at the front of the room, you can usually tell who is taking notes and who is writing a letter to their friend in Scotland.)

Ask questions

No, do not raise your hand to ask or answer questions every 90 seconds. Being an active listener means asking yourself if you understand everything that has been discussed. If the answer is no, ask the teacher questions at an appropriate time or write down questions that you must have answered to understand the subject fully.

Challenge yourself to draw conclusions from the things the teacher is saying. Do not just sit there letting your hand take notes. Let your mind do something, too. Think about the subject matter, how it relates to what you have been assigned to read and other facts to which you have been exposed.

To tape or not to tape

I am opposed to using a tape recorder as a substitute for an active brain in the classroom for quite a number of reasons.

- It is time-consuming. To be cynical about it, not only will you have to waste time sitting in the classroom, you will have to waste more time listening to that lesson again.

- It is virtually useless for review. Fast-forwarding and rewinding through cassettes to find the salient points of a lecture is too much trouble for too little benefit. During the hectic days before an exam, are you really going to want to waste time listening to a lecture when you can read so much more quickly?

- It offers no backup. Only the most diligent of students will tape record and take notes. So what happens if your tape recorder malfunctions? How useful will blank or distorted tapes be when it is time for you to review? If you are going to take notes anyway, as a method of backup, why not just do a good job note-taking and save yourself the time and effort of listening to that lecture over again?

- It costs money. Compare the price of blank paper and a pen to that of a tape recorder, batteries and tapes. The cost of batteries alone should convince you that you are better off on the low-tech route. (Save those batteries for your personal stereo.)

▌ You miss those 'live' clues discussed earlier. When all you
have is a tape of your lecture, you do not see that zealous
flash in your teacher's eyes, the passionate arm-flailing, the
stern set of the jaw, all of which should scream, 'Listen to
me – this will be in your exam'.

I do concede, however, that there are situations in which tape
recorders can be useful – such as when your head is so stuffed
up with a cold that 'active listening' during an hour-long lecture is virtually impossible. With this exception noted, I still
maintain that a tape recorder is no substitute for good listening skills.

What is 'chaff' anyway?

I am sure you have observed in your lessons that some people
are constantly taking notes. Others end up with two lines on
one page. Most of us fall in between.

The person who never stops taking notes is either writing a
letter to a friend in Scotland or has absolutely no idea what is
or is not important.

The results are dozens of pages of notes (by the end of the
term) that may or may not be helpful. This person is so busy
writing that he is not prepared or even aware that he can ask
and answer questions to help himself understand the material
better. To use that old adage, 'He can't see the wood for the
trees'. He is probably the same person who takes a marking
pen and underlines or highlights every word in the book.

Contrast him to the person who thinks note-taking is not
cool, so he only writes down today's date and the homework
assignment. He may write something when the teacher says,
"Now, write this down and remember it", but he probably just
scribbles some nonsense words. After all, he is cool.

Watch him sweat when it is time to study for the exam. He is
stuck with a faulty memory and a textbook that may not contain half the material that will be on the exam paper.

Taking concise, clear notes is first and foremost the practice
of discrimination – developing your ability to separate the essential from the superfluous, the key concepts, key facts, key

ideas from all the rest. In turn, this requires the ability to listen to what your teacher is saying and copying down only what you need to in order to understand the concept. For some, that could mean a single sentence; for others, a detailed example will be the key.

Just remember: the quality of your notes usually has little to do with their length – three key lines that reveal the core concepts of a whole lecture are far more valuable than paragraphs of less important data.

Even if you find yourself wandering helplessly in the lecturer's wake, so unsure of what she's saying that you cannot begin to separate the important, noteworthy material from the nonessential verbiage, use the techniques discussed in this chapter to organise and condense your notes anyway.

Tkng grt nts in clss

You know the year Columbus 'discovered' America. You know the chemical formula for oxygen. You also know Shakespeare wrote *Romeo and Juliet*. So why waste time and space writing them down?

Frequently, your teacher presents material that is commonly known in order to set the stage for further discussion or to introduce material that is more difficult. Do not be so conditioned to copy dates, vocabulary, terms and names, that you mindlessly scribble down information you already know.

Items discussed during any lesson could be grouped into several categories, which vary in importance.

■ Information not contained in the course texts and other assigned readings.

■ Explanations of obscure material covered in the texts and readings but with which students might have difficulty.

■ Demonstrations or examples that provide greater understanding of the subject matter.

■ Background information that puts the course material in context.

As you are listening to a teacher, decide which of these categories best fits the information being presented.

Develop your shorthand skills

You do not have to be good at shorthand to streamline your note-taking. Here are five ways.

1 Eliminate vowels. As a sign that was ubiquitous in London Underground stations used to proclaim, 'If u cn rd ths, u cn gt a gd jb'. (If you can read this, you can get a good job.)

2 Use word beginnings ('rep' for representative) and other easy-to-remember abbreviations.

3 Stop putting full stops after abbreviations. (They add up.)

4 Use standard symbols in place of words. Here is a list that will help you in most of your classes (you may recognise many of these symbols from maths and logic):

≈	Approximately
w/	With
w/o	Without
wh/	Which
→	Resulting in
←	As a result of/consequence of
+	And or also
*	Most importantly
cf	Compare; in comparison, in relation to
ff	Following
<	Less than
>	More than
=	The same as
↑	Increasing
↓	Decreasing

esp	Especially
$\triangle$	Change
$\subset$	It follows that
$\therefore$	Therefore
$\because$	Because

5 Create your own symbols and abbreviations based on your needs and comfort level.

There are two specific symbols you may want to create as they will be needed again and again.

(W) This is my symbol for 'What?', as in 'What on earth does that mean?' 'What did she say?' or 'What happened? I am completely lost!' It denotes something that has been missed – leave space in your notes to fill in the missing part of the puzzle after the lesson.

(M) This is my symbol for 'My idea' or 'My thought'. I want to clearly separate my own thoughts during a lecture from the lecturer's – put too many of your own ideas (without noting that they are yours) and your notes begin to lose some serious value.

Feel free to use your own code for these two important instances; you certainly do not have to use mine.

While I recommend using all the 'common' symbols and abbreviations listed previously all the time, in every lesson, so as to maintain consistency, you may want to create specific symbols or abbreviations for each course. In chemistry, for example, 'TD' may stand for thermodynamics, 'K' for the Kinetic Theory of Gases (but do not mix it up with the 'K' for Kelvin). In history, 'PM' is the prime minister, 'WC' is Winston Churchill, and 'FR' could be French Revolution (or 'freedom rider').

How do you keep everything straight? Whatever happens, summarise your abbreviations of each lesson's notes, perhaps on the front page in a corner, or create a list on the first page of that lesson's notebook or binder section for the abbreviations and symbols you intend to use regularly throughout the term.

Expanding on your 'shorthand'

While you are listening to the lecturer, you should be thinking about what you write down. Lectures are filled with so many words that will not be at all helpful when you sit down to study for your finals. Writing those words down and missing some of the truly important points of the lecture is counterproductive: your notes may look impressively complete, but what are they completely full of? All the important stuff or…?

For instance, if your teacher says, "The harsh terms of the Treaty of Versailles and the ineffectiveness of the Weimar Republic were two of the most prevalent themes in the early speeches of Hitler", you could write down something like:

Erly Hitler speeches: *hrsh Versailles Trty, Wmr wknss.

If the Treaty of Versailles is something that has been discussed frequently in class, you might write 'Vrs'. Continue to abbreviate more frequently as more terms become readily recognisable. In that way, the speed and effectiveness of your note-taking will increase as the academic year moves along.

I have also noticed that many students are prone to write big when they are writing fast and to use only a portion of the width of their paper. I suppose they think that turning over pages quickly means they are taking good notes. All it really means is that they are taking notes that will be difficult to read or use when it is review time. Force yourself to write neatly and take advantage of the entire width of your note paper.

But is it good for you?

Do you think this sort of shorthand will work for you? Probably not at first. When I worked as a reporter, I found that I could not trust my notes, at least not at first. But in trying to write so much down I also discovered that I could not trust my note-*taking*. As I gained more experience, however, my note-taking became more and more productive.

Be careful – in your fervour to adopt my shorthand system, do not abbreviate so much that your notes are absolutely unintelligible to you almost as soon as you write them.

The point here is, you must come up with a note-taking short-hand system that makes sense to you. You may certainly choose to abbreviate less and write a little more. Whatever system you develop, ensure it serves the right purpose: giving you the time to really listen to your teachers, rather than only furiously scribbling down what they say.

Draw your way to good marks

The one problem with this whole note-taking system I have been discussing is that many people find it more difficult to remember words rather than pictures, especially those who, on the 'My Ideal Study Environment' chart in Chapter 2, claimed they received information best visually rather than orally.

Problem solved: mapping is another way to take notes that stresses a more visual style – drawing or diagramming your notes rather than only writing them down.

Let me show you how to map the first few pages of this chapter as an example. Start with a clean sheet of paper and, boxed or circled in the centre, write the main topic.

How do you want your picture to read – top to bottom, bottom to top, clockwise in a circle, counterclockwise? I am going to set mine up from top to bottom. After deciding on the first major topic ('Utilising skills depends on lesson format') and placing it on your map, add the detail:

How to excel in the classroom

Lectures (emphases: listening, note-taking)

Discussions (emphases: asking/answering, analysing, discussing)

Combination (emphases: as above)

Hands-on (emphases: development/application pertinent skills)

Utilising skills depends on lesson format

The second major topic ('Know your teacher') and those that follow take their place in the line or circle you have chosen, in the direction you have chosen. I have completed a map containing four major topics on page 107.

Active participation: a 'Grade A' approach

In many tutorial and seminar groups, you will find that discussion, mostly in the form of questions and answers, is actively encouraged. This dialogue serves to both confirm your knowledge and comprehension of specific subject matter and identify those areas in which you need to work.

Whatever the format in which you find yourself, participate in any discussion to the best of your ability. Most teachers consider lesson participation a key ingredient in the marks they decide upon. No matter how many assignments and exams you sail through, if you never open your mouth in the classroom, you should not be surprised to get less than an A.

If you are having trouble following an argument or particular line of thought, ask for a review or for clarification.

Do not ask questions or make points hoping to impress your teacher – your real motive will probably be fairly obvious. Remember what you are there for – to learn the material and master it.

Based on the teacher's preferences and the classroom format, ask the questions you feel need answers.

Be careful you do not innocently distract yourself from practising your now excellent note-taking skills by starting to analyse something you do not understand or, worse, creating mental arguments because you disagree with something your teacher or a classmate said. Taking the time to mentally frame an elaborate question is equally distracting. All three cause the same problem: you are not listening.

Finally, listen closely to the words of your classmates. Knowledge has no boundaries, and you will often find their comments, attitudes and opinions as helpful and insightful as your teacher's.

What if you are shy or become tongue-tied whenever you are called on? Ask a question rather than taking part in the discussion – it is easier and, over time, may help you break the ice and jump into the discussion. If you really cannot open your mouth without running a fever, consider reading some books on how to gain confidence in public speaking.

Most importantly, prepare and practise. Fear of standing at the front of a classroom or even participating from the safety of your seat is, for many of you, really a symptom of lack of confidence.

This lack of confidence stems from lack of preparation. The more prepared you are – if you know the material back to front – the more likely you will be able to, even want to, raise your hand and 'strut your stuff'. Practising with friends, parents or relatives may also help.

If you are having trouble with oral reports, they are covered separately in Chapter 8. I think you will find the hints I have included there will eliminate much of the fear such talks seem to engender.

What to do after the lesson

As soon as possible after your lesson, review your notes, fill in the 'blanks', mark down questions you need to research in your text or ask during the next lesson and remember to mark any new assignments on your weekly calendar.

I tend to discourage recopying your notes as a general rule, since I believe it is more important to work on taking good notes the first time round and not waste the time it takes to recopy. But if you tend to write fast and illegibly, it might be a good idea to rewrite your notes so they are readable, taking the opportunity to summarise as you go. The better your notes, the better your chance of capturing and recalling the pertinent material.

This is why I recommend 'one period on, one off' – an open period, even half an hour, after each lesson to review that lesson's notes and prepare for the next one. It is not easy for most secondary school students to do, but at college and university you have a greater say in scheduling your tutorials and seminars.

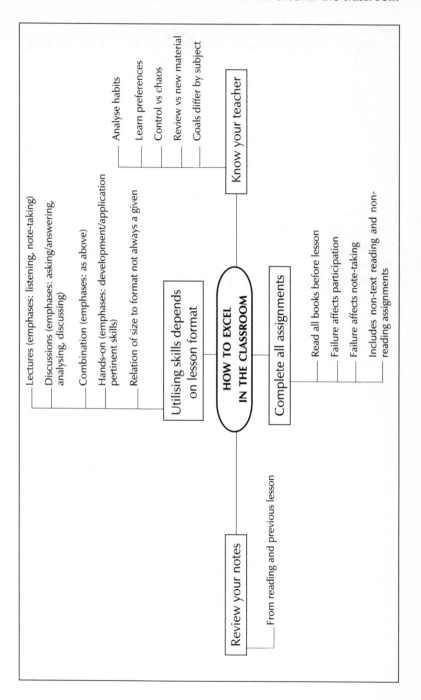

HOW TO EXCEL IN THE CLASSROOM

Utilising skills depends on lesson format
- Lectures (emphases: listening, note-taking)
- Discussions (emphases: asking/answering, analysing, discussing)
- Combination (emphases: as above)
- Hands-on (emphases: development/application pertinent skills)
- Relation of size to format not always a given

Know your teacher
- Analyse habits
- Learn preferences
- Control vs chaos
- Review vs new material
- Goals differ by subject

Complete all assignments
- Read all books before lesson
- Failure affects participation
- Failure affects note-taking
- Includes non-text reading and non-reading assignments

Review your notes
- From reading and previous lesson

How to use your library

Libraries contain the written record of humankind's brief stay on Planet Earth. They stand unparalleled as one of our finest accomplishments and unchallenged as reference and research sources. In your attempt to develop lifelong study skills, you will find yourself using the library constantly. It presents a single well from which we can draw knowledge and material throughout our lifetimes… without ever worrying about it running dry.

Libraries are in most towns large and small across the country and represent an amazingly democratic aspect of our culture. Rules and restrictions vary from library to library – public versus university, large versus small – but school, college and university students usually have access to virtually all library materials. Do not forget the best part: these services are free. A library card is your ticket to the world of knowledge that could keep you busy for the rest of your life.

Where to find a library

Start with your local phone directory to find your nearest library. As well as the public libraries, there are university and college libraries. As a college or university student, these are the ones you are most likely to use.

Also, of course, as we will discuss in the next chapter, you can access nearly any library in the world from the comfort of your own home. All you need is a computer, a modem and a service provider to surf the Net.

Many major university libraries dwarf all but the largest public library systems. If you have access to a major university library, consider it your good fortune and take advantage of it.

How libraries work

Most libraries are divided into reading rooms, restricted collections and unrestricted book sections. Unrestricted book sections are those through which anyone using the library can wander, choosing books to use while in the library or, if allowed, to take home. Restricted areas generally include any special collections of rare books, those open only to academics or to those with particular credentials, either by library rule or by order of whoever donated the collection (and, often, the room housing it). In some libraries, all book sections are closed, and all books must be obtained from a librarian.

Most libraries contain both circulating materials – those books and other items you may borrow and take home with you – and non-circulating materials – those that can be used only in the library. All fiction, general nonfiction and even most educational titles will usually be found in the first group. Reference material, periodicals and books in special collections are usually in the second.

A look at a national library

The British Library is the national library of the United Kingdom and one of the world's greatest research libraries. It offers a wider range of reference, document supply, bibliographic and information services than any other national library.

At the time of writing (spring 1997), the British Library is undergoing the biggest move in history. Over the next two years, books, manuscripts, sound recordings and other items from eleven buildings around London will be moved to a new, purpose-built building in St Pancras.

Three hundred kilometres of shelving will hold over 150 million separate items – a collection that has been developed over 250 years. The new library will provide 1206 seats for readers, whose access to the sources held by the library will be aided by three linked automated systems, the Online Public Access Catalogue (OPAC), holding 12 million records.

What can you find in the British Library? Almost anything you could want, including books, journals, manuscripts, maps, stamps, music, patents, newspaper and sound recordings in all written and spoken languages. Most of the material at the British Library is for reference only, hence the eleven reading rooms in the new St Pancras building! The library also offers enquiry and information services, literature searches and document supply services. Admission to all reading rooms is free, although for the more specialised areas you will need to apply for a pass.

But if you think the British Library is a place only suitable for quiet research, then think again. The events programme includes lectures, films and talks on a wide variety of topics. There are a number of permanent and special exhibitions, and workshops and study days are arranged for schools and adult learners. The Library offers its own training and consultancy services, and produces a wide variety of publications sold through its own Library Bookshop.

How a library is organised

To provide organisation and to facilitate access, most libraries utilise the Dewey Decimal Classification System, which uses numbers from 000 to 999 to classify all material by subject matter. It begins by organising all books into 10 major groupings:

000–099	General	500–599	Science
100–199	Philosophy	600–699	Useful Arts
200–299	Religion	700–799	Fine Arts
300–399	Social Sciences	800–899	Literature
400–499	Language	900–999	History

Given the millions of books available in major libraries, just dividing them into these 10 groups would still make it quite difficult to find a specific title. So each of the 10 major groupings is further divided into 10 and each of these 100 groups is assigned to more specific subjects within each large group. For example, within the Philosophy classification (100), 150 is psychology and 170 is ethics. Within the history classification (900), 910 is travel and 930 is ancient history.

There is even further subdivision. Mathematics is given its own number in the 500 (Science) series – 510. But specific subjects within mathematics are further classified: 511 is arithmetic; 512, algebra, and so on.

Finally, to simplify your search for materials even further, the last two digits in the Dewey Decimal code signify the type of book:

01 Philosophy of

02 Outlines of

03 Dictionary of

04 Essays about

05 Periodicals on

06 Society transactions and proceedings

07 Study or teaching of

08 Collections

09 History of

If your library does not use the Dewey system, it probably is organised using letters instead of numbers to denote major categories, for example:

A   General works (encyclopaedias and other reference)

B   Philosophy, Psychology and Religion

C   History – Auxiliary sciences (archeology, genealogy, etc)

D   History: General, non American

E   American history (general)

F   American history (local)

G   Geography / Anthropology

H   Social sciences (sociology, business, economics)

J   Political sciences

K Law

L Education

M Music

N Fine arts (art and architecture)

P Language/Literature

Q Sciences

R Medicine

S Agriculture

T Technology

U Military science

V Naval science

Z Bibliography/Library science

There are tens of thousands of new books published each year, and larger libraries will buy in quite a number. Books arrive almost daily and are sent to the cataloguing section for classification, special bindings (if needed) and shelf placement. Once entered into the system, books are indexed in the card catalogue (or, as is more often the case, in the computer) by author, title and subject matter. Finding a biography of Tolstoy, for example, is as easy as looking up Tolstoy in the card catalogue and copying down the appropriate codes for the particular one you want.

In a closed-shelf environment, you would give the appropriate numbers to a librarian and the books would be delivered to you. If the shelves are open, you have only to learn the way in which they are organised and search for your own books. Open shelf areas are often designated by letters of the alphabet (for fiction), by subject matter (in smaller libraries) or, in virtually all major libraries, according to the Dewey codes.

You may go to your local library and not even find a card catalogue, which might confuse you. Computers are taking over the world of business, so it is no surprise that a record-intensive 'business' like the library is in the forefront of computerisation. Librarians I have spoken to in America estimate that by the year 2000, 95 per cent of all US libraries will be online – with user friendly computer terminals replacing old-fashioned cards. Many libraries – maybe yours – are already online.

You do not have to leave home to access some of the greatest libraries in the world via the Internet, for example the entire US Library of Congress. All 110 million items currently housed on 500 miles of shelving will be available on the Internet by the year 2000. A lot of information is already on the Net, including early films of New York, special exhibitions from the Vatican Library and Dead Sea Scrolls and more.

Where to start

Feeling overwhelmed by the piles of volumes, classification systems, card catalogues and computers? You still have no excuse for not taking advantage of your library. All you have to do – if at all confused about tracking down the information you need – is ask the librarian.

Where to look for materials

You should review as wide a variety of reference materials as possible.

But how do you find out whether anyone has written a magazine or newspaper article about your topic? How do you know if there are any government documents or pamphlets that might be of help? How do you find those written-by-the-experts reference books?

Look in your library's publication indexes. These indexes list all of the articles, books and other materials that have been published and/or are available in your library.

I have listed some of the major publication indexes below. There are many others, so remember to ask your librarian for additional suggestions.

1 **The card catalogue.** This is a list of all the books in your library. (Stored on computer, it is still often called a card

catalogue because it used to be kept on index cards.) Books are indexed in three different ways: by subject, author and title.

2 **Newspaper indexes.** Many newspapers provide an indexed list of all articles they have published.

3 **Periodical indexes.** To find out if any magazine articles have been published on a particular subject, go to a periodical/journal index.

4 **Vertical file.** This is where you will find pamphlets and brochures.

5 **HMSO catalogue.** Useful for finding government publications.

Many libraries print lists of their resources and maps of where they can be found. What if yours does not? That's right... just ask your librarian for help – that is what he or she is there for.

Your approach to research

All of us who have become familiar with the wonders of the library have probably developed our own approach to enjoying its amenities and using them most efficiently.

My own experience emphasises what may already be obvious: getting the right start is all-important. Since I try to keep from becoming overwhelmed with material, I start any research working with the broadest outlines or topics (and the broadest resources) and wind my way down the ladder, getting more and more specific in topic and sources as I go.

Let us assume your assignment is to prepare a report on the current state of affairs in Bosnia. This is how you might approach the task.

1 Consult any one of the numerous leading encyclopaedias you will find in your library – *Britannica, Americana, Collier's, World Book,* etc. Here you will find an overview and historical perspective on the area. Encyclopaedic entries are

usually the most comprehensive and concise you will find. They cover so much territory and are so (relatively) up-to-date that they are an ideal 'big-picture' resource. Of course, when you are dealing with a relatively late-breaking news story such as that of Bosnia, you may find any encyclopaedia is woefully out of date. (Did you remember to look up 'Yugoslavia' to get some historical perspective?)

2 With overview to hand, you can start consulting the major indexes and directories your library has to develop a list of more specific resources. Obviously, the entries in these major resources can then be directly consulted – specific issues of daily broadsheet newspapers on microfilm, periodicals at the periodicals desk, etc. In no time at all, you will develop a long list of names and places to check, leading you to a number of potential topics and sources. Here is just a brief list of those you could cull from a single magazine or newspaper article, all relating to Bosnia: Ahja Izaetbegovic, Bosnia and Herzegovina, Croatia, Franjo Tudjman, Serbia, Slobodan Milosevic, Montenegro, Radovan Karadzic, Bosnian Serbs, Bosnian Croats, Ratko Mladic, Posavina Corridor, Eastern Slavonia, Muslims, Sarajevo, Belgrade and Dayton, Ohio. Do you think you will run out of research materials?

In one brief tour of your library's resources, you will easily discover and know how to obtain more material than you would need to write a book on virtually any one of the subtopics, let alone a report encompassing all of them.

What if you feel uncomfortable in the library? An infrequent user? Or simply find it a confusing place that is more trouble than it is worth? As I have emphasised, developing any habit is just a matter of practice. The more you use the library, the more comfortable you will feel using it. In a very short time, you will have your own list of resources that you start with whenever you receive an assignment.

If you want the library to become like a second home, its every shelf a familiar friend, why not work there? Many libraries, smaller ones in particular, often offer opportunities for paid and volunteer work. Even if you work for free this is an excellent way to learn the ins and outs of your library.

Many of you might not use the library as much as you should (or would like to) because it seems like a confusing series of catacombs. The more comfortable you are – the more you know about the materials it contains and how to find and use them – the more you will want to be there. And the more help you will be able to get from this superb resource.

7 How to use your computer

Using a computer is like having a dialogue. It is a one-way dialogue, with you asking questions and issuing orders, and your talking partner responding without complaint. It is a wonderful way of communicating except for two small drawbacks: you and your partner speak totally different languages, and neither of you hears what the other is saying. It is these little problems that make computers seem so mysterious and difficult to use. But remember: operating your computer is just like having a chat with a friend. All that hardware – those boxes, hard drives, chips, ports, busses, expansion slots, the screen, the keyboard and the mouse – are only there to make that simple conversation possible.

Whether you have the latest high-tech equipment or an older PC balancing precariously on your desk, you can use your computer to increase your skills, expand your knowledge and make research simple. Your computer can help you to:

▌ Brush up on your English skills.

▌ Increase and test your knowledge of mathematics, including algebra and geometry.

▌ Listen to native speakers pronouncing words in the language you are studying.

▌ Research issues in numerous encyclopaedias, dictionaries and other reference sources.

▌ Get information on abortion, civil rights and other issues from the organisations involved.

▌ Travel down the Amazon River, visit ancient Greek ruins or the site of a concentration camp.

▌ Read classical literature and philosophy in its original language or in English.

▌ Dissect the human body or watch as a virus invades a body cell.

▌ Pose questions to other students or professionals in the field you are studying.

▌ Study paintings in the Louvre and many other museums around the world.

▌ Read abstracts and complete articles from professional journals published around the world.

▌ Study the Magna Carta, the text of Dr Martin Luther King's 'I Have a Dream' speech or the latest party political manifestos.

▌ View blueprints of significant buildings.

▌ Practise for GCSE, A-level and other important exams and tests.

▌ Leave messages for and get information from the Prime Minister, government departments and government officials, or from the President of the United States.

▌ See the stars and the planets through the 'eyes' of spacecraft, satellites and probes.

▌ Study time lines of history, literature, physics and just about any other subject.

Once you have gathered all that information, you can use word processing programs such as Microsoft Word or WordPerfect to correct your spelling and grammar, to help you find more interesting words to use and to prepare professional-looking documents complete with italicised and bold typeface, columns and inserts.

For maths or accounting projects, you can use spreadsheet programs such as Excel or Lotus 1-2-3 to organise and manipulate data, and to prepare charts and graphs that illustrate the main points you want to make.

Database programs, which help you keep track of large bodies of information, can make gathering and organising information for a paper simplicity itself. Graphics programs help even the artistically challenged sketch out drawings and plans. Multimedia programs that combine text, video, sound and pictures can help you present what you have learned in a dynamic, compelling manner.

With various word processing, spreadsheet, database, graphics and multimedia programs, with educational and special-topic programs, with access to online and Internet services, the computer-aided student has a definite lead in the race to educational success.

Computers will not study for you or make you more clever, but they can make learning much more enjoyable, efficient and productive.

Buying the right computer

You may think mastering computer jargon and developing a general understanding of computers and what they can do for you is the hard part. As many of you know, actually buying the machine is often more difficult. With so many types of computers and peripherals available, made by many manufacturers, it can be difficult to decide which is best for you.

The countless different computers, screens, printers, hard drives and other devices lining the shelves can make a visit to the computer store both baffling and intimidating. There are so many things to consider: do you want to become part of the Macintosh world or the IBM world? If it is IBM, do you want an actual IBM machine, a Packard Bell, a Compaq, a Dell or one of any number of other IBM clones? Should you buy a black and white monitor, a colour monitor, a VGA colour monitor or a super VGA? Is a 500 MG hard drive enough? What about the Pentium?

Asking yourself the right questions

Begin the buying process by deciding what you want your computer to do, then finding the software that will do it. Only then should you look for the hardware to run that software. Long before thinking about which brand of computer or how many megs of RAM you need, ask yourself these 11 questions.

1 What are you going to use the computer for?

2 What software are you likely to use?

3 What kind of hardware does it take to run that software?

4 How much memory do you need to run your software?

5 What sort of hardware does your school/college/university use?

6 Where will you be using the computer?

7 How are you going to protect your files?

8 How much can you afford to spend?

9 Will you pay more for a recognisable brand name, or do you want to save money with a lesser-known company?

10 How much time do you want to spend setting up and configuring your computer?

11 Does the manufacturer of the computer you are considering offer service and support?

Some final tips before you buy

▮ Shop around. You will find computers in computer stores, computer 'super' stores, electronic stores, department stores and large discount warehouses.

■ Get written quotes, and make sure that everything you want is included in the quote.

■ Do not be afraid to haggle. Prices are rarely fixed, and you can often negotiate a better deal.

■ Find out if the computer you want is in stock, or if you have to wait for delivery.

■ Ask whether or not the store offers ongoing help on what they sell, or if you have to go to the manufacturer if a problem arises.

■ Tell the salesperson that you want your system software and other key programs pre-installed by the store – especially if you are a computer novice.

■ Go elsewhere if the salespeople do not answer your questions. If they are not helpful before they get your money, how helpful will they be once they do?

Finding the right software

Software is the key to computers; without it, all of that expensive hardware cannot do anything.

The programs (software) that you purchase and plug into your hardware are really only directions to the computer, nothing more than 'instruction books' written in code that the computer can understand.

Ah, but what those instruction books can make a computer do! They can fill your screen with the complete works of many authors, along with pictures and commentary. They can ask you hundreds of questions, then give you the answers, to help you prepare for exams such as GCSEs and A-levels. They can 'speak' to you in French and many other foreign languages so that you can hear how the language is supposed to sound. They can take you on tours of foreign countries, lands under the seas, battlefields and the inner workings of the human body. They can play music, show you famous artwork and recite poetry. They can, in short, be superb educational assistants.

When deciding whether to buy educational software, remember the following.

■ There is no such thing as the 'best' program in any educational category. Some are filled with complex information, while others focus on a few simplified concepts. Some rely heavily on text, while others delight you with sounds, pictures, videos and games. Some are aimed at younger students, while others are for the more advanced. Some are plain looking and straightforward, others high tech and glitzy. Which one is best? The one that best serves your needs.

■ You can find much of this same information on the Internet or through the online services, and information on a computer disk can quickly become dated. However, there is nothing like having what you need, right to hand, when you need it.

■ Your school or college may already have software you like in the classrooms or computer laboratory. See what it has to offer before buying your own.

■ It is best not to rely solely on the advertising copy you read on software boxes. Talk with your friends and read software reviews before parting with your money.

■ You must check the side of the software box for hardware requirements to make sure your computer can run the software. Be wary of 'minimum' and 'suggested' RAM requirements. In most cases, the suggestion is really a requirement.

Going online

Going online is easy, correct? All you have to do is master a few concepts and techniques, and learn the difference between the Information Superhighway, the Internet, Mosaic, Gopher, the Web, WATS, BBSes, servers, browsers, online services and ISPs.

Going online puts a tremendous amount of information at your fingertips. It is especially helpful to students, as it gives them access to a mind-boggling array of educational and research facilities, including:

▮ Hundreds of journals and magazines.

▮ Daily and weekly newspapers from around the country.

▮ Encyclopaedias.

▮ Bulletin boards.

▮ Education programs.

▮ Online 'teachers' who personally answer questions.

▮ Internet access to information sites filled with documents, statistics, lists and bibliographies on such subjects as abortion, affirmative action, animal rights, art, astronomy, aviation, biology, business/economics, chemistry, civil liberties, computers, criminology, food, dance, demography, domestic violence, feminism, film, genealogy, genetics, government, health, history, human rights, international affairs, literature, magic, mathematics, military, physics, places at home and abroad, politics, religion, space, theatre, weather – and just about anything else you can think of.

▮ Mini-courses in maths, English, physics, American history and most other subjects.

▮ Information about GCSE and A-level examinations and other tests, plus practice tests.

▮ Information about hundreds of colleges and universities, their admission requirements, student demographics and costs.

▮ Information on financial aid.

▌ An opportunity to 'chat' with other students.

▌ The ability to contact experts in every field, many of whom will take the time to answer questions or engage in debates.

And much more. New online features make it possible for you to request information on any subject. Think of all the time and effort you will save.

Before you begin surfing

Going online simply means hooking your computer up to another computer – or to many others – and allowing them to communicate with each other. You have 'lined up' your computer with another so that the information can flow. You can go online by:

▌ Physically running a cable between your computer and someone else's.

▌ Connecting computers via the telephone. If you connect over the phone wires, you will need a modem to convert the computers' signals into a form that can travel through the phone system.

Once online, you can begin cruising the Information Superhighway, also known as the Global Information Highway, the Information Highway, the info highway, The Highway and cyberspace.

What kind of information is on the Information Superhighway? Almost everything. Universities and research centres are online. So are government departments and local government offices, libraries, planetariums, newspapers, magazines, museums, political parties, sports teams, gardening clubs and pop groups' fan clubs, just to mention a few.

The amount of information on the superhighway is literally limitless, because you can use the highway to 'speak' to millions of other people via computer. Countless experts and amateurs in all fields are online, and many will allow you to take information out of their computers, or will answer your questions.

'Road maps'

Many 'road maps' to the Internet and other parts of the information highway have been developed, making it easy even for a novice to zip from information site to information site. For example, the World Wide Web, also known as the web or WWW, was developed as a navigational 'map' of the Internet, helping people to find what they are looking for. Other programs, such as Mosaic and Netscape, also help you browse (search) the Net.

Linking up to the Internet is easy. You simply go online through an Internet Service Provider (ISP), a company that puts your computer in touch with the others (for a fee). Students may be able to tap into the Internet via their school or college computers.

You can also plug into the Internet by way of commercial (for profit) online services such as CompuServe, Demon Internet, AOL UK, Delphi, Uunet Pipex and many others that are constantly being set up.

A quick look at some online services

Millions of people have signed up with commercial online services. Although limited, these 'package tours' are generally easy to use and offer a variety of other services, including news, educational information, financial information, entertainment and shopping.

There are a vast number of Internet service providers in the UK, and new ones appearing all the time. The following is a very brief random selection of national providers.

AOL, www.aol.com
BT Internet, www.btinternet.com
CompuServe, www.network.compuserve.com
Demon Internet, www.demon.net
Domino Systems, www.domino.com

Easynet, www.easynet.co.uk
FirstNet, www.firstnet.co.uk
GreenNet, www.gn.apc.org
Net Online, www.n-e-t.co.uk
Planet Internet, www.uk.pi.net
Planet Online, www.theplanet.net
Research Machines, www.rmplc.co.uk
TExNET, www.texnet.co.uk/texnet.html
Uunet Pipex, www.uunet.pipex.com
WinNet, www.win-uk.net
Xara Networks, www.xara.net
Zetnet, www.zetnet.co.uk

Among these Demon Internet is the UK's largest Internet provider. Established in 1992 it has now over 90,000 subscribers all over Europe. Demon Internet's biggest competitor is CompuServe, which is worth mentioning particularly for its education centre.

CompuServe

You can visit CompuServe's educational department through Sprynet, which offers you very good services to get the most out of the Internet. It provides you with quick classes to teach yourself some of the basics of the Internet and there is a tour to take to test what you have learned. Sprynet has a bookstore that gives you the opportunity to purchase a book from its list, and to chat and meet others and submit your favourite books. Sprynet has a library and a virtual university site. The latter offers you a variety of online classes, workshops and focus groups, in which nearly a quarter million people from 128 countries have already participated.

CompuServe gives you also a chance to meet online people who have similar interests, through a meeting place called The Forum. You can join a chat by simply entering a room and joining in a conversation to chat away about anything that interests you.

AOL UK

Another excellent educational provider is AOL (American Online) UK. Originally a large American network service, AOL is now becoming very popular in the UK. Some of its interesting features for students are as follows.

Life: Cliques and communities – everything from the teenagers to Third Agers. There are also many specialist community groups.

Weather: You can look at the whole country forecast, or zoom in on your particular area.

Travel: The travel channel offers guides to several countries and can be very useful to plan journeys.

Entertainment: This is where you'll find TV, film, music and other entertainment.

Finance: From home finance to worldwide stock quotes. Also *European Business News* and *Money Wise* magazines can be found online.

News: A constantly updated news feed keeps you up to date with the images and stories of the moment. AOL also has several newspapers online including *The Independent, The Mirror* and *Sunday Mirror* together with *Sporting Life* and some others.

Computing: Software libraries and reviews, user groups, information about computer companies and hardware, online edition of *Personal Computer World* magazine.

Internet: All about the Internet and the Internet Services that AOL launches. Net magazine online.

Chat: Enter chat rooms where you can discuss an incredible variety of subjects over the computer.

Learning: This is a channel devoted to knowledge – it houses all the reference materials AOL keeps online, as well as providing discussion areas for members who want to share each other's knowledge.

International: Access to all the AOLs in the world, games and multilingual chat.

These are just some of the resources available on AOL UK. Now let us look at the educational resources available on the Internet itself.

Surf's up on the Internet

The Internet – that vast, mysterious collection of computer networks linking every corner of the globe – is a cornucopia of facts, statistics, documents, opinions, arguments, lists, video and sound clips. The answer to almost any question is on the Internet – somewhere. The trick is to find it. There is no room in this book to list even a smattering of pertinent Internet sites but wherever you go on the Net, here are a few point to remember.

- Some of the sites are informative and well organised, some are quirky and skimpy.

- Some are well researched and trustworthy, and some can be the ravings of a mad person. Just because you see it on your computer screen does not mean that it is the truth.

- Some provide unbiased information with no ulterior motive, some slant their information to persuade you to their cause. Some are just offering enough information to entice you to buy something.

- Some are easy to use, some require you to search through listings to find what you need.

■ Some have the information, some link you to other sites and some are simply listings of sites.

■ Some may be gone when you look for them again. That sometimes happens.

■ Some are free, but some you have to pay for, and cost a lot. Be sure to check on the cost before going online.

Online services

Again, it is helpful to ask your teachers or friends about the online services they use. The cost can really vary between the different services on offer, so make sure you subscribe to the one that suits you and your pocket

The final word

Your computer and the world it can open for you is a wonderful tool and a fabulous adventure. Just remember that it is only a tool, and works much better if you have already developed all the other study skills in this book.

8 How to write excellent essays

It is going to happen, whether you like it or not. Sooner or later, you will have to prepare written and/or oral reports for virtually every one of your courses. If you are like most students, your reaction will be the same every time: 'Why me? What do I do? Where do I start?'

Reading this chapter will not make into you such a good writer that you can leave college or university and start visiting bookshops to preen in front of the window displays featuring your latest best seller.

However, there is really no reason to fear a written assignment or oral report, once you know the simple steps to take and rules to follow to complete it satisfactorily. Once you realise that 90 per cent of preparing an essay has nothing to do with writing... or even being able to write. And once you are confident that preparing essays by following my suggestions will probably get you a mark or two higher than you had before... even if you think you are the world's poorest excuse for a writer.

Doing a project assignment requires a lot of work. But the pay-off is excellent, too. You will learn, for example:

1 How to track down information about any subject.

2 How to sort through that information and come to a conclusion about your subject.

3 How to prepare an organised, in-depth report.

4 How to communicate your ideas clearly and effectively.

Once you develop these skills, you own them.

You will be able to apply them to all your secondary school, college or university lectures, not only when you prepare other project assignments, but also when you tackle smaller writing projects, such as essays and oral reports.

When you leave college or university, these same skills will help you get ahead in the working world; the ability to analyse a subject and communicate through the written word are keys to success, no matter what career you choose.

The skills you acquire as you learn how to produce your project assignment will be among the most valuable things you will learn while in education.

Five basic rules of essay writing

Let us start with the fundamental rules that need to be emblazoned on your wall.

1 *Always* follow your teacher's directions to the letter.

2 *Always* hand in your essay on time.

3 *Always* hand in a clean and clear copy of your essay.

4 *Never* allow a spelling or grammatical error in your essay.

5 *Always* keep at least one copy of every essay or assignment you write.

You wanted it typed?

Your teacher's directions may include:

■ A general subject area from which topics should be chosen – 'some aspect of Henry VIII's reign', 'a 19th-century invention', 'a poem by Wordsworth', etc.

■ Specific requirements regarding the format – typed, double-line spaced, include title page, do not include title page, etc.

■ Suggested length – eg, 10–15 typewritten pages.

▌ Other requirements – hand in general outline before the topic is approved; get verbal approval on your topic before proceeding; do not include quotes (from other works) longer than a single paragraph; other idiosyncrasies of your own teachers.

Whatever his or her directions, follow them to the letter. School teachers may be somewhat forgiving, but I have known university lecturers who simply refused to accept a written assignment that was not prepared exactly as they instructed – and gave the poor but wiser student an F for it (without even reading it).

If you are unsure of a specific requirement or if the suggested area of topics is unclear, it is your responsibility to talk to your lecturer and clarify whatever points are confusing you.

It is also not a bad idea to choose two or three topics you would like to write about and seek his or her preliminary approval if the assignment seems particularly vague – this way, you will know definitely that you are fulfilling the topic requirement.

So then my dog chewed the essay...

As you have studied and memorised Chapter 4, there is certainly no reason, short of catastrophic illness or life-threatening emergency, for you ever to be late with an assignment. Again, some teachers will refuse to accept an essay that is late. At best, they will mark you down for your lateness, perhaps turning an A essay into a B... or worse.

Is that coffee stain worth a B?

Teachers have to read a lot of essays and should not be faulted for being human if, after hundreds of pages, they come upon your coffee-stained, pencil-written tome and get a bit discouraged. Neither should you be surprised if they give you a lower mark than the content might merit just because the presentation is so poor.

I am not advocating 'form over substance'. Far from it – the content is what the teacher is looking for, and he or she will primarily be basing your mark on what you write. But presentation is important. So follow these simple rules.

I Never handwrite your written assignment.

I If you are using a word processor or word-processing program on your computer, use a new ribbon in your dot matrix printer and/or check the toner cartridge in your laser printer. If you type (or someone else types) your essay, use clean white bond and (preferably) a new carbon ribbon so that the images are crisp and clear.

I Unless otherwise instructed, always double-line space a typewritten essay.

I Use a simple typeface that is clear and easy to read; avoid those that are too big – stretching a five-page essay to 10 – or too small and hard to read.

I Never use a fancy italic, modern or any other ornate or hard-to-read typeface for the entire essay.

Use your old assignments as maps

There should be a number of helpful messages in your returned assignments or essays, which is why it is so important to retain them. What did your lecturer have to say? Are there comments applicable to the essay you are writing now – poor writing, lack of organisation, lack of research, bad transitions between paragraphs, poor grammar or punctuation, misspellings? The more of these comments – and, one would expect, the lower the marks – the more extensive the 'map' your lecturer has given you for your next assignment, showing you exactly where to 'locate' your A.

If you got a low mark but there are not any comments, perhaps you should have asked the teacher why you got such a poor mark? You may get the comments you need to make the next essay better. You will also be showing the teacher you actually care, which could help your marks the next time round.

Many employers happily use résumés and covering letters with grammatical and/or spelling errors for darts practise. Do not expect your teachers to be any more forgiving – there are definitely a few out there who will award an F without even noticing that the rest of the essay is great; hard luck if you misspelled 'Constantinople' or left a participle twisting slowly in the wind.

The Fry essay-writing system

The more complex a task or the longer you need to complete it, the more important your organisation becomes. By breaking down any written project assignment into a series of manageable steps, you will start to feel less chaotic, hectic and afraid right away.

Here are the steps that, with some minor variations along the way, are common to virtually any written report or assignment.

1 Research potential topics.

2 Finalise topic.

3 Carry out initial library research.

4 Prepare general outline.

5 Do detailed library research.

6 Prepare detailed outline (from note cards).

7 Write first draft.

8 Do additional research (if necessary).

9 Write second draft.

10 Spell-check and proofread.

11 Ask someone else to proofread.

12 Produce final draft.

13 Proofread one last time.

14 Hand it in and collect your A+.

Create a work schedule

Get out your calendar. Find the date on which your project assignment is due. How many weeks do you have until then? Plan to spend at least half of that time on research, the other half on writing.

Now, block out set periods of time during each week to work on your project. Schedule two- or three-hour chunks of work time, rather than many short periods, so you can really immerse yourself in your work.

As you make up your work schedule, set deadlines for completing various steps of your project. For example:

Week 1:   Decide on topic and 'angle' of your project.

Week 2:   Make list of references.

Weeks 3/4: Read reference materials; take notes.

Weeks 5/6: Do detailed outline; write first draft.

Week 7:   Edit assignment; prepare bibliography.

Week 8:   Proofread assignment; type final copy.

You should probably plan on consulting and/or taking notes from at least 10 different books, articles or other reference materials. (Your teacher or subject may demand more.) And you should plan on writing two or three drafts of your assignment before you arrive at the final copy.

Refer to your work schedule often, and adjust your speed if you find yourself lagging behind.

Steps 1 and 2: Consider and choose topic options

In some cases, your teacher will assign your topic. In others, your teacher will assign a general area of study, but you will have the freedom to pick a specific topic within that general area.

There are some pitfalls you must avoid. Let us say you need to write a 10-page essay for your history course, and you decide your topic will be 'The Industrial Revolution'. Can you really cover that in 10 pages? Not unless you simply rehash the high points, as in your third-year history book. You could write volumes on the subject (many people have) and still have plenty to say.

Instead, you need to focus on a particular, limited angle of your subject, such as, 'The Effect of James Hargreaves' Spinning Jenny on the Industrialisation of the North'.

However, you must not get too narrow in your focus. Choose a subject that is too limited, and you might run out of things to say on the second page of your essay. 'How a Spinning Jenny Works' might make an interesting one- or two-page story. It will not fill 10 or 15 pages.

Pick a topic that is too obscure, and you may find that little or no information has been written about it. Therefore, you will have to conduct your own experiments, interview your own research subjects and come up with your own original data. Hint: If you cannot find a single book on your supposed topic, rethink it. While you could choose a topic that can be researched using magazine articles, the newspaper, monographs, etc, why make your life so difficult if you do not have to?

Make sure there is enough research material available about your topic. Also ensure that there are enough different sources of material – different authors, different books, etc – so you can get a well-rounded view of your subject (and not be forced for lack of other material to find ways to make somebody else's points sound like your own).

Taking all of the above into consideration, do a little brainstorming now about possible topics for your project. Do not stop with the first idea – come up with several different possibilities. Put this book down until you have made a list of three or four potential topics.

How about trying to get two or more essays for two or more courses out of the same research? You may not be able to simply produce one essay for two courses, but with a little extra research – not what you would need to do for an entirely different assignment – you may well utilise a good portion of the first essay as the basis for a second. What an excellent way to maximise your library time.

Step 3: Begin initial library research

Take your list and go to the library. You need to do a little advance research. Scan your library's card-catalogue index and other publication indexes. See how many books and articles have been written about each topic on your 'possibilities' list. Next, read a short background article or encyclopaedia entry about each topic.

With any luck, you should be left with at least one topic that looks like a good research subject. If two or more topics passed your preliminary research test, pick the one that interests you the most. You are going to spend a lot of time learning about your subject. There is no rule that says you cannot enjoy it.

Develop a temporary thesis

Once you have chosen the topic for your project assignment, you must develop a temporary thesis. (The word 'thesis' is a relative of 'hypothesis' and means about the same thing – the central argument you will attempt to prove or disprove in your assignment. A thesis is not the same thing as a topic. Your topic is what you study; your thesis is the conclusion you draw from that study.)

A 'thesis statement' is a one-sentence summary of your thesis. It sums up the main point of your assignment.

Note that I said temporary thesis. It may not end up being your final thesis. As you have not completed all your research yet, you can only come up with a 'best-guess' thesis at this point.

If a temporary thesis does not spring easily to mind – and it may not – sit back, and do some more brainstorming. Ask yourself questions like:

- What is special or unusual about _____? (Fill in the blank with your topic.)

- How is _____ related to events in the past?

- What impact has _____ made on society?

- What do I want the world to know about _____?

- What questions do I have about _____?

Step 4: Create a temporary outline

Once you have developed your temporary thesis, give some thought as to how you might approach the subject in your project. Jot down the various issues you plan to investigate. Then, come up with a brief, temporary outline of your project, showing the order in which you might discuss those issues.

Do not worry too much about this outline – it will be brief, at best. It is simply a starting point for your research, a plan of attack. But do not skip this step, either, as it will be a big help in organising your research findings.

Step 5: do detailed library research

We have already reviewed the library and how to take advantage of its resources. Now, let us talk about exactly how you will keep track of all the resources and information that you will gather for your project assignment.

To create your working bibliography, you will need a supply of 3x5 inch index cards. You will also use index cards when you take notes for your assignment, so buy a big batch now – about 300 cards ought to be sufficient. At the same time, pick up one of those little envelope files designed to hold the cards. Put your name, address and phone number on the file. If you lose it, some kind person can return it.

Before you do anything else, send away for anything you want to review that is not available in your library. If you need a brochure from a particular association, for example, order it now as it may take a few weeks for such materials to arrive. (Check the online services and Internet to see if any needed material can be easily downloaded. The more skilled Web browsers among you may spend little on postage, even for obscure material from Zimbabwe.)

Start a systematic search for any materials that might have information related to your project. Look through the indexes we covered in Chapter 6 and any other indexes your librarian recommends.

When you find a book, article or other resource that looks promising, take out a blank note card. On the front of the card, write down the following information:

In the upper right-hand corner of the card: The library classification number (Dewey decimal number or other classification system number), if there is one. Add any other details that will help you locate the material on the library shelves (Science Reading Room, Reference Room).

On the main part of the card: The author's name, if given – last name first, first name, middle name/initial. Then the title of the article, if applicable, in quotation marks, followed by the name of the book, magazine, newspaper or other publication – underlined.

Add any details you will need if you have to find the book or article again, such as the date of publication, edition, volume number and page numbers on which the article or information appears.

In the upper left-hand corner of the card: Number it. The first card you write on will be No. 1, the second, No. 2, and so on. If you inadvertently skip a number somewhere along the line, do not worry. It is only important that you assign a different number to each card.

At the bottom of the card: If you are going to be researching in more than one library, write the library's name. Also write down the name of the index in which you found the resource, in case you need to refer to it again.

Do this for each potential source of information you find and put only one resource on each card.

Sample bibliography card for a book

```
(1)                                    315.6
                          Main Reading Room


               Jones, Karen A


          The Life and Times of Bob Smith
               (see esp pp 43-8)


                  Card Catalogue
               High Street Library
```

Sample bibliography card for a magazine article

```
(2)                              Periodical Room


               Perkins, Stan
        'The Life and Times of Bob Smith'
                 Smith Magazine
          (24 April, 1989; pp 22-6)


                 Readers' Guide
               University Library
```

Sample bibliography card for a newspaper article

```
(3)                                    Microfiche Room


                        Black, Bill
             'Bob Smith: The New Widget Spinner'
                        The Times
             (16 June, 1976, late ed, p A12)


                      The Times Index
                     High Street Library
```

Citing online information

Because students are increasingly using online sources, the Modern Language Association of America, which publishes style guides for research papers, has integrated electronic citations into its latest edition.

An example of an online citation:

Terhune, Alan J 'Sensationalism' *Reporting News*
http://www.ccs.syr.edu/home/lbp/reporting-news.html (22 May 1995)

Now hit the books

Set aside solid blocks of time for your library work. It is better to schedule a handful of extended trips to the library than 15 or 20 brief visits. When you go to the library, take your bibliography cards, a good supply of blank index cards, your preliminary outline and several pens or pencils.

Your bibliography cards serve as the map for your information treasure hunt. Get out a stack of five or six cards, and find the materials listed on those cards. Set up camp at a secluded desk or table and start working.

When you write your assignment, you will get all the information you need from your notes, rather than from the original sources. Therefore, it is vital that you take careful and complete notes. What sort of information should you put in your notes? Anything related to your subject and especially to your thesis. This includes:

1 General background information (names, dates, historical data, etc).

2 Research statistics.

3 Quotes by experts.

4 Definitions of technical terms.

You may be used to keeping your notes in a ring binder or notepad. I am going to show you a better way – recording all of your notes on index cards.

For example, you have found a reference book that contains some information about your subject. Before you begin taking notes, get out the bibliography card for that book.

Check that all of the information on your card is correct. Is the title exactly as printed on the book? Is the author's name spelled correctly? Add any other information you need to include in your final bibliography.

Note-taking guidelines

Once your bibliography card is completed, set it aside. Get out some blank index cards and start taking notes from your reference source following these guidelines.

▮ **Write one thought, idea, quote or fact on each card**. If you encounter a very long quote or string of data, you can write on both the front and back of a card, if necessary. But never carry a note to a second card.

▌ **Write in your own words**. Summarise key points about a paragraph or section. Avoid copying things word for word.

▌ **Put quotation marks around any material copied verbatim**. It is acceptable to include in your essay a sentence or paragraph written by someone else to emphasise a particular point (providing you do so on a limited basis). But you must copy such statements exactly as written in the original source – every word, every comma, every full stop.

Adding detail to your note cards

As you finish each note card, do the following:

▌ **In the upper left-hand corner of the card**, write down the resource number of the corresponding bibliography card (from its left-hand corner). This will remind you where you found the information.

▌ **Below the resource number**, write the page number(s) on which the information appeared.

▌ **Get out your preliminary outline**. Under which outline topic heading does the information on your card seem to fit? Jot the appropriate topic letter in the upper right-hand corner of your note card.

If you are not sure where the information fits into your outline, put an asterisk instead of a topic letter. Later, when you do a more detailed outline, you can try to fit these 'miscellaneous' note cards into specific areas.

▌ **Next to the topic letter**, jot down a one- or two-word 'headline' that describes the information on the card.

▌ **When you have finished taking notes from a particular resource**, put a tick on the bibliography card. This will show you that you have finished with that resource, at least for now.

Make sure that you transfer information accurately to your note cards. Double-check names, dates and other statistics. As with your bibliography cards, it is not so important that you put each of these elements in the exact places I have outlined above. You just need to be consistent. Always put the page number in the same place, in the same manner. Do the same with the resource number, the topic heading and the headline.

Add your personal notes

Throughout your note-taking process, you may want to make some 'personal' note cards. On these cards, jot down any thoughts, ideas or impressions you may have about your subject or your thesis.

Write each thought on a separate note card, as you have with the information you have taken from other resources, and also assign your note card a topic heading and mini-headline. In the space where you would normally put the number of the resource, put your own initials.

Step 6: Prepare a detailed outline

Your research is complete.

This means that at least one-half of your assignment – perhaps as much as three-quarters of it – is done, even though you have still to write one word of the first draft.

It is time to organise your data. You need to decide if your temporary thesis is still on target, determine how you will organise your assignment and create a detailed outline.

This is where the note-card system really pays off. Your note cards give you a great tool for organising your work. Get out all of your note cards, then:

1 Group together all the cards that share the same outline topic letter (the letter in the right-hand corner of each card).

2 Put these different groups in order, according to your temporary outline. (Put all of your topic A cards at the front of the pack of cards, followed by topic B cards, then topic C cards, etc.)

3 Within each topic group, sort the cards further. Group the cards that share the same 'headline' (the two-word title in the upper right-hand corner).

4 Go through your miscellaneous topic cards, the ones you marked with an asterisk. Can you fit any of them into your existing topic groups? If so, replace the asterisk with the topic letter. If not, put the card at the very back of your pack.

Your note cards now should be organised according to your preliminary outline. Take a few minutes to read through your note cards, beginning at the front of the pack and moving through to the back. What you are reading is actually a rough sketch of your project – the information you have collected in the order you plan to present it in your assignment. Does that order make sense? Would another arrangement work better?

Here are some of the different organisational approaches you might consider for your assignment.

1 **Chronological.** Discuss events in the order in which they happened (by time of occurrence).

2 **Spatial.** Present information in geographical or physical order (from north to south, largest to smallest, etc).

3 **Cause/effect.** One by one, discuss the effects of a series of individual events or actions.

4 **Problem/solution.** Present a series of problems and possible solutions.

5 **Compare/contrast.** Discuss similarities and differences between people, things or events.

6 **Order of importance.** Discuss the most important aspects of an issue first and continue through to the least important.

If necessary, revise your general outline according to the organisational decision you have made. Next, go through each group of cards that share the same topic letter. Rearrange them so that they, too, follow the organisational pattern you chose.

After you have sorted all the cards that have been assigned a specific topic heading (A, B, C, etc), review the cards that are marked with an asterisk. Try to work out where they fit in your pack of cards.

Now flip through your note cards from front to back. Look! You have created a detailed outline without even knowing it. The topic letters on your note cards match the main topics of your outline; and those headlines on your note cards are the subtopics for your outline.

Simply transfer your note card headlines to paper. They appear on your outline in the same order as they appear in your pack of cards.

Step 7: Write the first draft

You may not have realised it, but you have already done a lot of the hard work that goes into the writing stage. You have thought about how your written assignment will flow, you have organised your notes and you have prepared a detailed outline. All that is left is to transfer your information and ideas from note cards to paper.

Good writing takes concentration and thought; concentration and thought require quiet – and lots of it. You also need to have plenty of desk space, so you can spread out your note cards in front of you; your work area should be well lit and you should have a dictionary and thesaurus close at hand. If possible, work on a computer, so you can add, delete and rearrange your words at the touch of a button.

Remember: at this point, your goal is to produce a rough draft – with the emphasis on the word 'rough'. Your first draft is not supposed to be perfect. It is supposed to need revision.

However, your thoughts, ideas and logic are the foundation of your assignment. And you need to build a foundation before you worry about hanging the front door. So, for now, only concentrate on getting your thoughts on paper. Do not worry about using exactly the 'right' word. Do not worry about getting commas in all the right places. We will take care of all that polishing later.

Your note cards helped you come up with a detailed outline. Now, they are going to help you plot out the actual paragraphs and sentences of your essay.

1 Your note cards should be arranged in the same order as your detailed outline. Take out all of the note cards labelled with the letter of the first topic in your outline.

2 From these, take out all the cards marked with the same 'headline' as the first subheading in your outline.

3 Look at the information on those cards. Think about how the various pieces of information might fit together in a paragraph.

4 Rearrange those cards so they fall in the order you have determined is best for the paragraph.

5 Do this for each group of cards, until you reach the end of the pack.

Each paragraph in your assignment is like a mini-essay. It should have a topic sentence – a statement of the key point or fact you will discuss in the paragraph – and contain the evidence to support it. This evidence can come in different forms, such as quotes from experts, research statistics, examples from research or from your own experience, detailed descriptions or other background information.

Construct each paragraph carefully, and your readers will have no choice but to agree with your final conclusion.

Now put it all on paper

Turn your note-card draft into a written rough draft. Using your cards as your guide, sit down and write.

Double- or triple-line space your draft, so that it will be easy to edit later on. After you have finished with a note card, put a tick at the bottom of the card.

If you decide that you will not include information from a particular card, do not throw the card away... yet. Keep it in a separate pile. You may decide to fit in that piece of information in another part of your assignment. Or you may change your mind after you read your rough draft and decide to include the information after all.

Help for when you get stuck

Got writer's block already? Here are a few tricks to get you unstuck.

- Pretend you are writing a letter to a good friend, and tell him or her everything you have learned about your subject and why you believe your thesis is correct.

- Use everyday language. Too many people try to use fancy words and phrases and forget that their goal is communication. Simpler is better. Drop the 'pound' words and settle for the 'pence'.

- Type something. Once you have written that first sentence – even if it is really bad – your brain will start to generate spontaneous ideas.

- Do not edit yourself. As you write your rough draft, try to remember your goal at this point is just a rough draft.

- Keep moving. If you become stuck on a particular section, do not sit there stewing over it for hours... or even many minutes. Just write a quick note about what you plan to cover in that section, and go on.

- If you cannot get even that much out, skip over the section altogether and come back to it later. Force yourself to go all the way through your essay, with as few stops as possible.

Document your sources

To avoid plagiarism, you must document the source when you put any of the following in your essays:

▌ Quotations taken from a published source.

▌ Someone else's theories or ideas.

▌ Someone else's sentences, phrases or special expressions.

▌ Facts, figures and research data compiled by someone else.

▌ Graphs, pictures and charts designed by someone else.

There are some exceptions. You do not need to document the source of a fact, theory or expression that is common knowledge.

You also do not need a source note when you use a phrase or expression for which there is no known author.

For a test of whether a statement needs a source note, ask yourself whether readers would otherwise think that you had come up with the information or idea all by yourself. If the answer is yes, you need a source note. If you are in doubt, include a source note anyway.

Footnotes

For many years, the preferred way to credit sources was the footnote. Two other forms of documentation, end-notes and parenthetical notes, are popular now as well.

A footnote is a source note that appears at the bottom of a page of text. You put a raised (superscript) number at the end of the statement or fact you need to document, which tells your readers to look at the bottom of the page for a note about the source of the data.

What goes in a footnote? The same information that is in the bibliography listing and the exact page number the information appears on.

In front of that source note, you put the same superscript number as you put next to the statement or fact in your text.

There is no limit to the number of footnotes you may have in your essay. Number each footnote consecutively, starting with the number 1. For every footnote 'flag' in your essay, make sure there is a corresponding source note at the bottom of the page.

Similar to bibliography listings, different authorities cite different rules for setting up footnotes. Ask your teacher whose rules you are to follow.

Step 8: Do additional research

Did you discover any gaps in your research when you wrote your first draft? Are there some questions which you will need additional information to answer? If so, now is the time to return to the library for one last go at the books.

Stop 9: Write the second draft

The goal for this phase is to edit for meaning – improve the flow of your essay, organise your thoughts better, clarify confusing points and strengthen weak arguments.

Focus on all of the problem areas you found. Add new data or information, if needed. Play with sentences, paragraphs and even entire sections. If you are working with a computer, this is fairly easy to do. You can change the order of words, cut and add sentences and rearrange whole pages with a few keystrokes.

If you are working with a typewriter or pencil and paper, you can do the same thing, but with scissors and tape.

As you review your rough draft, ask yourself the following questions.

▮ Do your thoughts move logically from one point to the next?

▮ Is the meaning of every sentence and paragraph crystal clear?

▮ Does every sentence make a point – or support one?

▮ Do you move smoothly from one paragraph to the next?

▪ Do you support your conclusions with solid evidence – research data, examples, statistics?

▪ Do you include a good mix of evidence – quotes from experts, scientific data, personal experiences, historical examples?

▪ Do you have a solid introduction and conclusion?

▪ Did you write in your own words and style, without merely stringing together phrases and quotes 'borrowed' from other authors?

▪ Have you explained your subject thoroughly? (Do not assume that readers have more knowledge about it than they actually do. Remember: you are familiar with the topic now, but you have spent weeks on it. Just because something is now 'obvious' to you does not mean your readers will know what you are talking about.)

▪ Have you convinced your readers that your thesis is valid?

When you have finished editing for content and meaning, print or type a clean copy of your essay, then double-check all of your facts for accuracy.

▪ Did you spell names, terms and places correctly?

▪ When you quoted dates and statistics, did you type in the numbers correctly?

▪ Do you have a source note (or preliminary source note) for every fact, expression or idea that is not your own?

▪ If you quoted material from a source, did you quote that source exactly, word for word, comma for comma, and did you put the material in quotation marks?

Mark any corrections on your new draft. Use a coloured pen or pencil so you will easily spot corrections later.

Now take an even closer look at your sentences and paragraphs. Try to make them smoother, tighter, easier to understand.

▌ Is it too wordy? Seize every opportunity to make the same point in fewer words.

▌ Are there places where phrasing or construction is awkward? Try to rearrange the sentence or section so that it has a better flow.

▌ Did you use descriptive, colourful words? Did you tell your reader 'The planes were damaged' or paint a more colourful and creative picture: 'The planes were broken-down hulks of rusted metal – bullet-ridden, neglected warbirds that could barely limp down the runway'?

▌ Consult a thesaurus for synonyms that work better than the words you originally chose.

▌ Have you overused particular words? Constantly using the same words makes your writing boring. Check a thesaurus for other possibilities.

▌ How do the words sound? When you read your essay aloud, does it flow like a rhythmic piece of music or plod along like a dirge? Vary the length of your sentences and paragraphs to make your writing more exciting.

▌ Always remember the point of the essay – to communicate your ideas as clearly and concisely as possible. So do not get lost in the details. Relax. If you have to choose between that 'perfect' word and the most organised essay imaginable, opt for the latter.

Again, mark corrections on your draft with a coloured pen or pencil. No need to retype your essay yet – unless it is so marked up that this makes it hard to read.

Step 10: Check your spelling and proofread

All right, this is the part that nearly everyone dislikes: it is time to rid your essay of any mistakes in grammar and spelling.

I have told you your thoughts are the most important element of your essay, which is true. However, it is also true that glaring mistakes in grammar and spelling will lead your teacher to believe that you are either careless or downright ignorant – neither of which will bode well for your final marks.

So get out your dictionary and a reference book on English usage and grammar. Scour your essay, sentence by sentence, marking corrections with your coloured pen or pencil. Look for the following.

- **Misspelled words**. Check every word. If you are using a spell-checking computer program, be careful of sound-alike words. 'There' might be spelled correctly, but not if you meant to write 'their'.

- **Incorrect punctuation**. Review the rules for placement of commas, quotation marks, full stops, etc. Make sure you follow those rules throughout your essay.

- **Incorrect sentence structure**. Look for dangling participles, split infinitives, sentences that end in prepositions and other various grammar no-no's.

Step 11: Ask someone else to proofread

Retype your essay, making all those corrections you marked during the last step. Format the essay according to the teacher's instructions. Incorporate your final footnotes and bibliography.

Give your project a title, one that is as short and sweet as possible, but tells readers what they can expect to learn from your project.

Find someone who is a good proofreader – a parent, relative, friend – and ask him or her to proofread your essay before you put together the final draft.

Steps 12, 13 and 14: The final draft

Incorporate any changes or errors your proofreader may have found. Type the final draft. Proofread it again – very carefully.

When everything is absolutely perfect, photocopy your paper. Every penny is worth paying to make a copy of your assignment. After all your hard work, you want to be sure you have a backup copy in case you lose or damage your original.

The last step. Put your assignment in a new manuscript binder, ring binder or folder. Then, hand it in on time, of course!

Oral reports

There are some key differences between writing a report and presenting it orally, especially if you do not want to make the mistake of just reading your report in front of the class.

If you have been assigned to give a talk for a class, it will probably fall into one of the following categories.

▪ **Exposition**: a straightforward statement of facts.

▪ **Argument**: trying to change the opinions of at least a portion of the audience.

▪ **Description**: providing a visual picture to your listeners.

▪ **Narration**: story-telling.

The most common forms of oral reports assigned in college or university will be exposition and argument. You will find that you will research and organise information for these types of speeches in much the same way as you would a termly assignment.

As you gather information for your report, making notes on index cards as you did for your project, keep this in mind: in order for you to be effective, you must use some different techniques when you tell your story rather than write it. Here are a few.

▮ Do not make your topic too broad. This advice, offered for preparing written reports as well, is even more important when preparing a talk. Try giving an effective speech on 'Shakespeare', '19th-century European politics' or 'Updike's novels' in 15 minutes – frequently the amount of time assigned for oral reports. These topics are more suited to a series of books.

'Rabbit and Babbit: Same character, different towns?', 'Disraeli and the British Empire' or 'Sex and sensuality in Shakespeare's sonnets' are more manageable. Narrowing the scope of your talk will help you research and organise it more effectively.

▮ Do not overuse statistics. While they are very important for lending credibility, too many will weigh down your speech and bore your audience.

▮ Anecdotes add colour and life to your talk, but use them sparingly, because they can slow down your speech. Get to the punch line before the yawns start.

▮ Be careful with quotes. Unlike a written assignment, a speech allows you to establish yourself as an authority with less fear of being accused of plagiarism. So you can present a lot more facts without attribution. (However, you should have the sources to hand in case you are asked about your facts.)

I have found that trying to shuffle a bunch of papers at the front of a classroom is difficult and that note cards that fit in the palm of your hand are a lot easier to use. But only if the notes on them are very short and to the point, to act as 'triggers' rather than verbatim cue cards – hanging on to 300 note cards is as difficult as a sheaf of papers.

Remember: you will actually be holding these cards in your sweaty palms and speaking from them, so write notes, not whole sentences. The shorter the notes – and the more often you practise your report so each note triggers the right information – the more effective your report will be. (The less you look at them makes eye contact with your classmates and teacher easier.)

Here are ways to make oral reports more effective.

∎ Pick out one person to talk to – preferably a friend, but an animated and/or interested person will do – and direct your talk to them.

∎ Practise, practise, practise your presentation. Jangled nerves are often the result of a lack of confidence. The better you know your material, the less nervous you will be and the better and more spontaneous your presentation.

∎ If you suffer from involuntary 'shakes' at the mere thought of standing in front of a roomful of people, make sure you can use a lectern, desk or something to hang on to.

∎ Take a deep breath before you go to the front of the classroom. Do not worry about pausing, even taking another deep breath or two, if you lose your place or find your confidence slipping away.

∎ If every trick in the world still does not steady your nerves, consider taking a public speaking course, joining the Toastmasters Club or seeking out similar extracurricular help.

How to study for exams

Tests. Mocks. GCSEs, A-levels, Finals. RSA, City and Guilds. Civil Service exams. Aptitude tests. Employment tests.

Throughout your educational life – and, more than likely, the rest of your life – testing will be an inevitable if sometimes frightening and distressing reality. The sooner you learn the techniques of preparing for, taking and mastering tests and exams, the better off you will be.

What do they want to know?

Many exams are as much a measure of the way you study – your ability to organise a mountain of material – as they are a measure of your knowledge of the material itself. This is especially true of any exam that purports to measure knowledge spread across the years and your mastery of such a broad spectrum of material – such as bar or medical exams; exams for nurses, accountancy exams, financial planners, etc; or the three days of oral exams my own university put everyone through. This means the better you study, the better your marks will probably be on such exams.

There are, as we have already seen, ways to organise your studying to achieve maximum results in minimal time. There are a great number of such techniques to use when studying for tests of any kind.

Before you can decide how to study for a particular test or exam, it is imperative that you know exactly what you are being tested on. Preparing for a weekly test is very different from preparing for a degree's final exam.

Studying for a psychometric test that many organisations use as an initial weeding out of potential employees is also completely different – you cannot pull out your textbook and, knowing what chapters are being included, just revise.

The structure of the test is also of paramount importance, not necessarily in terms of how you study, but how you tackle it once you get your test paper.

What are you afraid of?

Before I start handing out exam-taking techniques, let us tackle one of the key problems many of you will face – exam anxiety, that all-too-common reaction to exams characterised by sweaty palms, a blank mind and the urge to flee to Pago Pago on the next available cargo ship.

What does it mean when someone proclaims she does not 'test well'? It may mean she does not study well (or, at the very least, prepare well). Or it could mean she is easily distracted, unprepared for the type of test she is confronting or simply unprepared mentally to take any test (which may include mentally sabotaging herself into getting poor marks, even though she knows the material inside out).

Take heart – very few people look forward to an exam; more of you are afraid of them than you would think, but that does not mean you have to fear them.

Since we all recognise the competitive nature of tests, being in the right frame of mind when taking them is important. Some of us rise to the occasion when facing such a challenge. Others are thrown off balance by the pressure. Both reactions probably have little to do with one's level of knowledge, relative intelligence or amount of preparation. The brightest students in your class may be the ones most afraid of exams.

Generally speaking, the best way to avoid the pitfalls of the extraordinary pressures of a testing situation is to place yourself in that environment as often as possible. Yes, practice helps. Get permission from your teachers to retake some past exams to practise the test-taking techniques and exorcise the High Anxiety Demon. Take a couple of standardised tests that your careers office might have, too, as the fill-in-the-box answer sheets and questions on the printed form have their own set of rules.

There are also some surprisingly simple steps you can take to give yourself the edge by being less on edge.

Dealing with exam anxiety

Few people enter an examination room cool, calm and ready for action. Most of us have various butterflies gambolling in our stomachs, sweat glands operating in overdrive and a sincere desire to be somewhere else... anywhere else.

Even if you are just entering secondary school, you have a few years of tests under your belt and should have some idea of how well or poorly you react to a test situation. If the answer is 'not well', start trying some of the following options until you find the one(s) that work for you.

'I know I can, I know I can'

The more pressure you put on yourself – the larger you allow an exam (and, of course, your hoped-for good marks) to loom in your own mind – the less you are helping yourself. (Also the bigger the exam really is, the more likely you are to keep reminding yourself of its importance.)

No matter how important an exam really may be to your career – and, let us face it, your marks on some can have a major effect on where you go to university, whether you get the job you want – it is just as important to de-emphasise that exam's importance in your mind. This should have no effect on your preparation – you should still study as if your life depended on a superior score. It might.

A friend of mine signed up to take a law school admissions exam, not just once, but twice. The first time, he did 'OK, not great'. By the time the second date arrived, he had come to his senses and decided not to become a lawyer. But as he had already paid for the thing, he took the exam again anyway. Are you ahead of me? That's right – 15 per cent improvement with no studying.

Keeping the whole experience in perspective might also help. Twenty years from now nobody will remember, or care, what you scored on any exam – no matter how life determining you feel that exam is right now.

Of course, you can make it easier by not going out of your way – certainly before an especially big or important exam – to add more stress to an already stressful life. Two days before your finals is not the time to dump a boyfriend, change your accommodation, take out a big loan or create any other waves in your normally placid river of life.

How to lower your AQ (anxiety quotient)

To come to terms with the 'importance' of an exam, read the list below. Knowing the answers to as many of these questions as possible will help reduce your anxiety.

1 What material will the exam cover?

2 How many total points are possible?

3 What percentage of my course marks are based on this exam?

4 How much time will I have to take the exam?

5 Where will the exam be held?

6 What kinds of questions will be on the exam (matching, multiple-choice, essay, true/false...)?

7 How many marks will be assigned to each question? Will certain types of questions count more than others? How many of each type of question will there be on the exam?

8 Will it be an open-book exam?

9 What can I take in with me? Calculator? Sweets? Other material crucial to my success?

10 Will I be penalised for wrong answers?

Hit the road, Jack

You have already found that scheduling breaks during your study routine makes it easier for you to focus on your books and complete your assignments faster and with more concentration. Scheduling breaks during exams has the same effect.

No matter what the time limits or pressures, do not feel you cannot afford such a brief respite. You may need it most when you are convinced you can least afford it, just as those who most need time management techniques 'just do not have the time' to learn them.

I'm relaxing as fast as I can!

If your mind is a jumble of facts and figures, names and dates, you may find it difficult to concentrate on the specific details you need to recall, even if you know all the material inside out. The adrenalin rushing through your system may just make 'instant retrieval' impossible.

The simplest relaxation technique is deep breathing. Lean back in your chair, relax your muscles and take three very deep breaths and count to 10 while you hold each one.

There are a variety of meditation techniques that may also work for you. Each is based on a similar principle – focusing your mind on one thing to the exclusion of everything else. While you are concentrating on the object of your meditation (even if the object is nothing, a nonsense word or a spot on the wall), your mind cannot be thinking about anything else and this allows it to slow down a bit.

The next time you cannot focus, try sitting back, taking three deep breaths and concentrating for a minute or two on the word 'Mu'. Afterwards you should be in a far more relaxed state and ready to tackle any exam.

If you feel this helps, consider learning some sort of meditation technique or even self-hypnosis.

Preparing for great exam results

Some rites of preparation are pertinent to any exam, from a weekly test to a final degree paper and everything in between.

Plan ahead

I admit it. When I was a student, even in college, my attention span tended to be bounded by weekends. Tell me in October that there would be a big exam in the first week of December and I would remember, probably, around 30 November.

Such habits lead to cramming, crib sheets and failed exams.

The key to avoiding all of these unpleasantries is regular, periodic review. The more often you review, the less often you will have to burn the midnight oil the week of the exam. If you have stayed on top of the material, written down and asked questions that arose from your reviews and reread lesson and textbook notes to make sure you understand everything, your last-minute review will be relatively leisurely and organised, not feverish and hassled.

Later in this chapter I will be talking about the possibility of forming a study group, which might make the review process even easier.

Use two alarm clocks

Doing badly in an exam is discouraging. Doing badly in an exam you felt ready for is depressing. Missing the exam entirely is devastating. It is essential that you know when and where all exams are scheduled and allow ample time to get to them.

If you are still in secondary school, getting to a particular exam should not be too hard – it will probably be held during your regular lesson period, in your normal classroom.

However, in colleges and universities exams may be scheduled at a different time to the normal lecture period... and at entirely different sites.

As soon as you know the time and location of any major exam enter it on your weekly calendar. Whether at secondary school, college or university, most of them set aside a week, two or even more for final exams. This exam period is usually clearly marked in your college or university handbook, announced in lectures (usually on the first day), printed on your course syllabus, etc.

Make optional assignments mandatory

Sometimes, in addition to your regular reading and other assignments, the teacher will assign optional reading at the beginning of a course. These books, articles, etc, may never be discussed in any lesson – but material from them may be included on a test, especially a final exam. If you have neglected to add this supplementary reading to your regular weekly assignments calendar, but wish to read it before the exam, make sure you allow enough time to buy or find these books. A lot of other students may also have left this reading to the last minute, and you may be unable to find the material you need if you wait too long.

Pens, pencils... sweets

Lastly, bring whatever materials you need to the exam, from pens and pencils to calculators. I also recommend, especially for a long test or a three-hour paper, that you take along some sweets, a chocolate bar or some other 'quick energy' snack to help wake you up when you need to give yourself a figurative slap in the face.

Although many exam papers will include room for notes, it may not be sufficient for your purposes. If you are asked to write three, five or even more essay questions, you will want a lot of scrap paper to outline and organise your thoughts before you put pen to paper. Similarly, a particularly complex maths test may quickly use up every square inch of margin. So bring along a separate writing pad or even a stack of scrap paper. There are few situations in which their use will not be allowed.

If you did not listen before...

Review, review, review. If you do not follow my advice for periodic review, you must be sure, especially for mid-terms and finals, to set aside the time to do the review and studying you need in the week or two before the exam.

The more material you need to review, the more important it is to clear your schedule. A four-, five- or six-course load covering 20, 40 or more books, lectures and discussions, essays and projects, easily generates hundreds of pages of notes. Reviewing, understanding and studying them will require your full-time effort for a week or even two. So make sure all other end-of-term work, especially major projects such as written assignments, are out of the way.

Whether you need to schedule a solid two weeks for a complete review or just two or three days because you have already reviewed most of your course work on a regular basis, make sure you schedule the time you have allocated on your weekly calendar, allowing more time for the subjects in which you are weakest, of course.

Why cramming does not work

We have all done it at one time or another, with one excuse or another – waited until the last minute and then tried to cram a week's or month's or entire term's worth of work into a single night or weekend. Did it work for you? I doubt it.

The reality is that cramming works at one level – for a small minority of students. Somehow, they are able to shove more 'stuff' into short-term memory than the rest of us and actually remember it, at least for 24 hours. After 24 hours? Gone with the wind. This means if they managed to do well on a weekly test, all that cramming was a waste of time for the mid-term exams or finals coming up. It certainly did not manage to affect at all what they actually learned from the course, and what they can carry with them in understanding and knowledge long after the course is just a memory.

The rest of us do not even get that smidgen of good news – after a sleepless night and too much coffee, we are lucky if we remember where the exam is the next morning. A couple of hours later, trying to stay awake long enough to make it back to bed, not only have we learned nothing, we have not even done very well on the exam we crammed for.

That is probably the best reason of all not to cram – it just does not work.

How to cram anyway

Nevertheless, despite your resolve, best intentions and firm conviction that cramming is a losing proposition, you may well find yourself – though hopefully not too often – in the position of needing to do something the night before a test you have not studied for at all. If so, there are some rules to follow that will make your night of cramming at least marginally successful.

Be realistic about what you do

You really cannot master an entire term's worth of work in a single night, especially if your class attendance has been sporadic (or nonexistent) and you have skimmed two books out of a syllabus of two dozen. The more information you try to cram in, the less effective you will be.

Needless to say, being realistic means a sober assessment of your situation – you are hanging by your thumbs and are just trying to avoid falling into the boiling oil. Avoiding the oil, saving the damsel in distress and inheriting the kingdom ('sailing through' the test) is a bit too much to ask for, no matter who is your fairy godmother. Also, of course, you are not expecting to remember anything about the course one day after the exam, are you?

Be selective and study in depth

The more you have managed to miss, the more selective you need to be in organising your cramming session. You cannot study it all. Use every technique in this chapter to separate the wheat from the chaff (or, at least, the ones you expect to be on the exam from the ones you do not). Then study the topics one by one, only moving to the second when you feel you have an excellent grasp of the first. It is better in this case to know a lot about a little rather than a little about a lot. You may get lucky and pick the three topics the three essays cover!

Massage your memory

Use every memory technique in this book to maximise what you are able to retain in your short-term memory. Repetition is key; reciting out aloud is a good idea.

Know when to give up

When you cannot remember your name, give up and get some sleep. Better to arrive at the exam with some sleep under your belt and feeling as relaxed as possible.

Consider an early morning rather than a late-night cram

Especially if you are a 'morning' person, but even if you are not, I have personally found it more effective to go to bed early and get up early rather than go to bed late and get up exhausted. Such a plan also lets you remember all this stuff for less time.

Spend the first few minutes writing down whatever you remember now but are afraid you will forget

A suggestion good at any time but especially when your mind is trying to hold on to so many facts and figures it seems ready to explode.

When in doubt, ask

Yes, there are teachers who will test you on the most mundane details of their course, requiring you to review every book, every note, every scribble.

I do not think many teachers work like this. You will more than likely be tested on some subset of the course, those particular topics or problems or facts or figures the teacher believes are the most important.

How do you know what those are? To put it bluntly, how do you know what is going to be on the exam paper? An important question, especially since I keep urging you to tailor and organise your studying based on such information.

Teachers give many clues. In general, the more often you see or hear the same material, the more important it probably is and the more likely it will show up on an exam paper. A subhead in your textbook repeated twice in the same lecture or class, repeated again just a week before the exam? What do you need, a megaphone announcing 'This is on the exam'?

A fact or topic need not be repeated in order to scream 'learn me'. Just as you learned to watch a teacher's body language and listen for verbal clues to identify noteworthy topics, you will also learn to identify topics which the teacher indicates – not verbally – are the most important. Your teacher's attitude towards note-taking may well tip you off, as well. If he or she asks you to take detailed notes – even wants them handed in (sometimes at secondary school but never at college or university) – I would suggest that your lesson notes are far and away more important than the textbook(s).

Have you saved earlier tests and exam papers from that course? Returned exams papers, especially if they contain a lot of comments from your teacher, should give you an excellent indication of where to concentrate your study time.

Is it wrong to ask the teacher what kind of test to expect? Absolutely not. Will he or she always tell you? Absolutely not. But it is not wrong to research that teacher's exams from previous years – students a year or two ahead of you can sometimes be of invaluable help in this effort.

Why? Like most of us, teachers are creatures of habit. While you certainly should not expect to find questions that will be duplicated, you can glean a few key things from previous exams, like the format the teacher seems to prefer and the areas that seem to be stressed. Do not take any of this for granted however: even creatures of the most set habits can turn over a new leaf now and then.

More list-making, please

Once you have discovered the type of exam facing you, you want to work out what is actually going to be on it (and, therefore, what you actually need to study). Remember: it is rarely, if ever, 'everything'.

In general, take the time to eliminate from consideration, with the possible exception of a cursory review, material you are convinced is simply not important enough to be included on an approaching exam. This will automatically give you more time to concentrate on those areas you are sure will be included.

Then create a 'To Study' sheet for each test. On it, list specific books to review, notes to recheck, specific topics, find concepts to go over, etc. Then tick off each item as you study it. This is akin to breaking the assignment-writing process into the 14 smaller, easier-to-accomplish steps and will have the same effect – to minimise procrastination, logically organise your studying and give you ongoing 'jolts' of accomplishment as you complete each item.

Test yourself

Just as you have made it a habit to write down questions as you study your textbooks, why not try to construct your own exams? The harder you make them, the better prepared and more confident you will be walking into the exam.

Practice tests offer some real advantages, whether you are studying for a weekly test, a GCSE or your bar exam. In fact, the longer and more 'standardised' the test, the more important it is to be familiar with its structure, its rules and its traps.

First and foremost, familiarisation with whatever type of exam you are taking is vitally important as it enables you to strategically study the material (prioritise) and strategically attack the exam (organise).

Familiarisation breeds comfort and, as I have pointed out more than once, being comfortable – relaxed – is a key component to doing well.

Familiarisation also breeds organisation, allowing you to concentrate on the exam itself and not on its structure. This gives you more time to actually take the exam rather than work out what it is about. It also reduces the effect of whatever time restraints the test imposes on you. The greater the time restraints, the more practicing will enable you to deal with them in the actual exam, minimising the pressure.

Last but not least, doing practice exams is a highly effective way to study and remember the material.

Exam-day rules and reminders

If the exam is not simply during a regular lesson period, make sure to arrive at the exam room early. Based on your preferences (from Chapter 2), sit where you like.

Be careful, however. There may be some variations you have to take into account. In an exam where there are 200 or 300 people in a room, there is a distinct advantage in sitting at the front: you can hear the instructions and the answers to questions better, and generally get the exam paper first.

Go all the way

Begin at the beginning. Then move through to the end. No, I am not talking about taking the exam, I am talking about looking through the exam paper or booklet and taking a glance at all the questions. If you have permission to go all the way through it, do that before you even start writing. Give yourself an overview of what lies ahead. This lets you spot the easier sections (and do them first) and get an idea of the marks assigned to each section.

Know the ground rules

Will you be penalised for guessing? The teacher, for example, may inform you that you will earn two points for every correct answer but lose one point for every incorrect one. This will certainly affect whether you guess or skip the question – or, at the very least, how many potential answers you feel you need to eliminate before the odds of guessing are in your favour.

Are the questions or sections weighted? Some exams may have two, three or more sections, some of which count for very little (10 or 20 per cent of your final marks) while one, usually a major essay, may be more heavily weighted (50 per cent or more of your marks). This should dramatically alter the amount of time you spend on each section.

Discriminate and eliminate

There is usually nothing wrong with guessing, unless, of course, you know that wrong answers will be penalised. Even then, as I have pointed out, guessing is not necessarily wrong. The question is how much to guess.

If there is no penalty for wrong answers, never leave an answer blank. But you should also do everything you can to increase your odds of getting it right. If every multiple-choice question gives you four possible answers, you have a 25 per cent chance of being right (and a 75 per cent chance of being wrong) each time you have to guess.

However, if you can eliminate a single answer – one you are reasonably certain cannot be right – your chances of being correct are 33 per cent.

If you can get down to a choice between two answers, it is just like flipping a coin: 50/50. In the long run, you will guess as many right as wrong. Even if there is a penalty for guessing, I would probably pick an answer if I had managed to increase my chances of getting the right one to 50/50.

Presuming you have managed to eliminate one or more answers but are still unsure of the correct answer and have no particular way to eliminate further, here are some real insider tips to make your guess more 'educated'.

▪ If two answers sound alike, choose neither.

▪ If the answers to a mathematical question cover a broad range, choose the number in the middle.

▪ If two quantities are very close, choose one of them.

▪ If two numbers differ only by a decimal point (and the others are not close), choose one of them.
  (Example: 2.3, 40, 1.5, 6, 15; I would go with 1.5 or 15. If I could at least work out from the question where the decimal point should go, even better.)

▪ If two answers to a maths problem look alike – either formulas or shapes – choose one of them.

Remember: this is not the way to 'sail through' an exam – these are just some tried-and-tested ways to increase your guessing power when you have absolutely nothing else to go on and nothing left to do.

What about going back, rechecking your work and changing a guess? How valid was that first guess? Surprisingly enough, statistics show it was probably pretty good (presuming you had some basis for guessing in the first place). So good that you should only change it if:

- It really was just a wild guess and, upon further thought, you conclude that the answer really should be eliminated (in which case your next guess is, at least, not quite so wild).

- You remembered something that changes the odds of your guess completely. (Even better, the answer to a later question helped you work out the answer to this one.)

- You miscalculated on a maths problem.

- You misread the question (did not notice a 'not', a 'never', an 'always' or some other important qualifier).

Guess and guess again?

If you do guess at any of the objective questions and you are getting your exam paper returned to you, place a little dot or other symbol beside them. This will let you know how successful your guessing was.

When you think you have finished a whole section, double-check to see if that is correct. Check again to make sure that all the questions have been answered.

It's a long race, so pace yourself

If you have 100 multiple-choice questions and you have 50 minutes allotted for that section, you do not have to be a first-class maths student to work out that you should spend a maximum of 30 seconds on each answer.

Do not depend on a wall clock to tell you the time. Take your own watch.

Answer every fourth question

Read and understand the directions. As I stressed in Chapter 8, you could appear to be doing everything right, but not follow your teacher's explicit directions, in which case everything is wrong.

If you are supposed to tick every correct answer to each question in a multiple-choice test – and you are assuming only one answer to each question is correct – you are going to miss a lot of answers.

If you are to choose one essay question out of three, or two out of five, that is very different from trying to answer every one. You will not do it. And even if you do, the teacher will probably only mark the first two. As you needed to allocate enough time to do the other three, it is highly doubtful that your first two answers will be so detailed and perfect that they will be able to stand alone.

Be aware of time. Again, if questions or sections are weighted, you will want to make sure you allow extra time for those that count the most. Better to do a superior job on the two sections that count for 90 per cent of the marks and dash through the 10 per cent section as the teacher is collecting the papers.

If there are pertinent facts or formulas you are afraid you will forget, write them down somewhere on your exam paper, or on scrap paper, before you do anything else. It will not take much time and it could save you some serious memory jogs later.

First out could be first failed

Leave some time at the end to recheck your answers.

Speaking of time, do not make a habit of leaving the exam room early. There is little to be gained from supposedly impressing the teacher and other students with how clever you (think you) are by being first to finish. Take the time to make sure you have done your best. If you are completely satisfied with your answers to all of the questions, it is fine to leave, even if you are first. But in general, slowing down will help you avoid careless mistakes.

Similarly, do not worry about what everybody else is doing. Even if you are the last person left, who cares? Everybody else could have failed, no matter how early and confidently they strode from the room. So take all the time you need and do the best you can.

16 tips for 'sailing through' multiple-choice tests

1 Be careful you do not read too much into questions. Do not try to second-guess the test setters, become too elaborate and ruin the answer.

2 Underline the key words.

3 If two choices are very similar, the answer is probably not either of them.

4 If two choices are opposite, one of them is probably correct.

5 Do not go against your first impulse unless you are sure you were wrong.

6 Check for negatives and other words that are there to throw you off.

7 The answer is usually wrong if it contains 'all', 'always', 'never' or 'none'. I repeat, usually.

8 The answer has a great chance of being right if it has 'sometimes', 'probably' or 'some'.

9 When you do not know the right answer, look for the wrong one.

10 Do not eliminate an answer unless you actually know what every word means.

11 Read every answer (unless you are wildly guessing at the last minute and there is no penalty).

12 If it is a standardised test, consider transferring all the answers from one section to the answer sheet at the same time.

13 If you are supposed to read a long passage and then answer questions about it, read the questions first. That will tell

you what you are looking for and affect the way you read the passage.

14 The longest and/or most complicated answer to a question is often correct.

15 Be suspicious of choices that seem obvious to a 2-year-old. Why would the teacher give you such a giveaway?

16 Similarly, do not give up on a question that, after one reading, seems hopelessly confusing or hard. Looking at it from a different angle, restating it in your own words, drawing a picture, etc, may help you realise it is not as hard as you first thought.

Test-taking strategies

In addition to some of the general ideas we have talked about, there are very specific strategies to use depending on the type of test you are taking. Let us look at them one at a time.

All of the above again?

There are three ways to attack a multiple-choice test.

1 Start at the first question and keep going, question by question, until you reach the end, never leaving a question until you have either answered it fully or made an educated guess.

2 Answer every easy question – the ones you know the answers to without any thinking at all or those requiring the simplest calculations – first, then go back and do the harder ones.

3 Answer the hardest questions first, then go back and do the easy ones.

None of these three options is inherently right or wrong. Each may work for different individuals. (I am assuming that these three approaches are all in the context of the test format. Weighted sections may well affect your strategy.)

The first approach is, in one sense, the quickest, in that no time is wasted reading through the whole test trying to pick out either the easiest or hardest questions. Presuming you do not allow yourself to get stumped by a single question so that you spend an inordinate amount of time on it, it is probably the method most of you use.

The second approach ensures that you will maximise your right answers – you are putting those you are certain of down first. It may also, presuming that you knock off these easy ones relatively fast, give you the most time to work on those that you find particularly difficult.

Many experts recommend this method because they maintain that answering so many questions one after another gives you immediate confidence to tackle the questions you are not sure about. If you find that you agree, then by all means use this strategy. However, you may consider just noting the easy ones as you preread the test. This takes less time and, to me, delivers the same 'confidence boost'.

The last approach is the one I used. In fact, I made it a point to do the very hardest questions first, then work my way 'down' the difficulty ladder. (This means I often worked backwards since many test setters and teachers make their tests progressively more difficult.)

It may sound strange to you, so let me explain the psychology. I worked out if time pressure starts getting to me at the end of the test, I would rather be in a position to answer the easiest questions – and a lot of them – in the limited time left, rather than the ones I really had to think about. After all, by the end of the test, my mind was simply not working as well as it was at the beginning.

That is the major benefit of the third approach: when I was most awake, most alert, I tackled questions that required the most analysis, thinking, interpretation, etc. When I was most tired – near the end – I was answering the questions that were virtually 'giveaways'.

At the same time, I was also giving myself a real shot of confidence. As soon as I finished the first hard question, I already felt better. When I finished all of the hard ones, everything was downhill.

However, I would always try to ensure adequate time to at least put down an answer for every question. Better to get one question wrong and complete three other answers than get one right and leave three blank. It is not the approach for everybody, but it may be right for you.

Do not fall into the answer daze, that blank stare some students get when they cannot think of an answer – for 10 minutes. Do something. Better to move on and get that one question wrong than waste invaluable time doing nothing.

50/50 odds are not bad: true or false?

What can you do to increase your scores on true-false tests?

First of all, be more inclined to guess if you have to. After all, I encouraged you to guess on a multiple-choice test if you could eliminate enough wrong answers to get down to two, one of which is correct. Well, you are already there. So, unless you are being penalised for guessing, guess anyway. (Even if you are being penalised, you may well want to take a shot at it if you have the faintest clue of the correct answer.)

What tricks do test setters incorporate in true-false tests? Here are three to watch out for.

Two parts (statements) that are true (or, at least, may be true) linked in such a way that the whole statement becomes false. Example: 'Since many birds can fly, they use stones to grind their food'. Many birds do fly, and birds do swallow stones to grind their food, but a causal relationship (the word 'since') between the two clauses makes the whole statement false.

On a multiple-choice test, the longest and/or most complicated answer to a question is often correct – the test setter has been forced to add qualifying clauses or phrases to make that answer complete and unequivocal. The exact opposite is true regarding true-false tests. The longer and/or more complicated a statement in a true-false test, the less likely it is to be true, as every clause of it must be true (and there are so many chances for a single part to be false).

Few broad, general statements are true without exception. Always be on your guard when you see the words 'all', 'always', 'no', 'never' or other absolutes. As long as you can think of a single example which proves such a statement false, then it is false. Be wary: there are statements with such absolutes that are true; they are just rare.

There are no 'easy' exams

Some people think 'open-book' exams are the easiest of all. They pray for them – until they see their first one.

These are the toughest tests of all, if only because even normally 'nice' teachers feel no compunction whatsoever about making such exams as tough as a sergeant-major on drill duty. Well, you can use your book! Many open-book exams are also homework tests, meaning you can use your notes (and any other books or tools you can think of).

Because you have to anticipate that there will be no easy questions, no matter how well you know the material, you need to do some preparation before this type of exam.

▋ Mark important pages by turning down corners, using paper clips or any other method that will help you turn quickly to important charts, tables, summaries or illustrations.

▋ Write an index of the pages you have turned down so you know where to turn immediately for a specific chart, graph, table, etc.

▋ Summarise all important facts, formulas, etc, on a separate sheet.

▋ If you are also allowed to bring your notes or it is a homework test, write a brief index to your notes (general topics only) so you know where to find pertinent information.

First, answer the questions for which you do not need the book, including those you are fairly sure of and those you know where to find. Star the latter ones.

Next, take out your book and check up on your starred answers and erase the stars once you have answered the questions. Then work on those questions for which you must rely fully on the book.

While a homework test is, by definition, an open-book exam, it is the hardest of all. An open-book exam in a lesson period simply cannot last longer than the time allotted for that lesson. A homework exam may give you a night or two, in some cases as long as a week, to complete.

Why are they so hard? You are given so much time because teachers expect that it will take you longer than the time available in the lesson to finish. You may have to go well beyond your text(s) and notes to even get a handle on some of the questions, leading to some long nights at the library. The longer you are given, the easier it is to procrastinate ('Well, I have got another two nights'), and we know where that leads.

There are only two good aspects to balance the scales. You have certainly been given the chance to 'be all that you can be'. No excuse for not doing a terrific job on a test with virtually no time limit. Also, if you tend to freeze during a normal exam, you should have far less anxiety at home in comfortable surroundings.

Write on!

While I think open-book tests are the hardest ones given, I must admit I think all 'objective' tests – including multiple-choice and true-false – are harder than essay exams. As I suspect many of you do not agree, let me explain.

I think an objective test of any kind gives the teacher much more latitude, even the option of focusing only on the obscurest details (which, granted, only the truly sadistic would do). As a result, it is much more difficult to eliminate areas or topics when studying for such a test (except, as discussed before, by using the clues the teacher has given you about the relative importance of certain topics and whatever your research into returned examination papers and those from previous years has turned up).

It is also rare to be given a choice – answer any 25 out of 50 – whereas you may often be given, for example, five essay questions and have to choose only three. This greatly increases the odds that even sporadic studying will have at least given you some semblance of understanding about one or two of the questions, whereas you may be lost on a 100-question true-false test.

Second, less can go wrong on an essay exam – there are only three or four questions to read, not 100 potential misreads. I could think of a few questions, not hundreds. I would have the time to organise (a strength) and I would probably gain points for good spelling, grammar and writing (another strength). It is also a lot easier to budget time between three or four essays than 150 multiple-choice questions.

Whether you love or hate essays, there are some important pointers to ensure you at least score better on them. Approach essay questions the same way as you would assignments. While you cannot check your textbook or go to the library to do research, the facts, ideas, comparisons, etc, you need are in your own cerebral library – your mind.

Here is the step-by-step way to answer every essay question.

■ **Step one:** on a blank sheet of paper, write down all the facts, ideas, concepts, etc, you feel should be included in your answer.

■ **Step two**: organise them in the order in which they should appear. You do not have to rewrite your notes into a detailed outline. Why not just number each note in the order you want to place it?

■ **Step three:** Compose your first paragraph, working on it just as long and as hard as I suggested you do in your assignments. It should summarise and introduce the key points you will make in your essay. This is where superior essay answers are made or unmade.

■ **Step four:** Write your essay, with your handwriting as legible as possible. Most teachers I have known do not go out of their way to decipher spidery handwriting masquerading as an essay and do not award high marks to it either.

▍ **Step five:** Reread your essay and, if necessary, add points left out, correct spelling, grammar, etc. Also watch for a careless omission that could cause serious damage – leaving out a 'not', making the point opposite to the one you wanted.

If there is a particular fact you know is important and should be included but you cannot remember it, guess if you can. Otherwise, just leave it out and do your best. If the rest of your essay is well thought out and organised and clearly communicates all the other points that should be included, I doubt if most teachers will mark you down too severely for such an omission.

Remember: few teachers will be impressed by length. A well-organised, well-constructed, specific answer to their question will always get you a better mark than writing down everything you know in the faint hope that you will actually answer the question correctly.

Think of the introduction and the conclusion as the bread in a sandwich, with the information in between as the cheese, lettuce, tomato and pickle. Everything is necessary for it all to hang together, but the main attraction is going to be what is between the slices.

Worry less about the specific words and more about the information. Organise your answer to a fault and write to be understood, not to impress. Better to use shorter sentences, paragraphs and words – and be clear and concise – than to let the teacher fall into a clausal nightmare from which he may never emerge (and neither will your A).

If you do not have the faintest clue what the question means, ask. If you really still have no idea of the answer – leave it blank. Writing down everything you think you know about the supposed subject in the hope that one or two things will actually have something to do with the question is, in my mind, a waste of everyone's time. Better to allocate the time you would waste to other parts of the exam and do a better job on those.

What if time runs out?

While you should have carefully allocated sufficient time to complete each essay before you started working on the first, things happen. You may find yourself with two minutes left and one essay to go. What do you do? As quickly as possible, do Steps one and two on page 179. If you then have time to reorganise your notes into a better organised outline, do so. Many teachers will give you at least some marks (sometimes nearly full marks) if your outline contains all the information the answer was supposed to. It will at least show you knew a lot about the subject and were capable of outlining a reasonable response.

One of the reasons you may have left yourself with insufficient time to answer one or more questions is that you knew too much about the previous question(s), and you wanted to make sure the teacher knew you knew, so you wrote and wrote and wrote… until you ran out of time.

Be careful – some teachers throw in a relatively general question that, if you wanted to, you could write about until next week. In that case, they are not testing your knowledge of the whole subject as much as your ability to edit yourself, to organise and summarise the important points.

Read the instructions and question carefully. If you are supposed to 'compare and contrast', do not just compare. If you are to analyse, do not only summarise. If you are supposed to discuss three key reasons something occurred, do not stop at two. In fact, I would go out of my way to underline each key point in any essay that requires a specific number of ways, reasons, explanations, or whatever, to make sure a tired teacher does not miss one and mark you down for it.

Index